D1241722

RACISM
AND THE CHRISTIAN
UNDERSTANDING OF MAN

Racism and the Christian Understanding of Man

by GEORGE D. KELSEY

CHARLES SCRIBNER'S SONS, New York

A–10.65 [V]

PRINTED IN THE UNITED STATES OF AMERICA

Library of Congress Catalog Card Number: 65-27241

TO LEOLA

Preface

Racism is a faith. It is a form of idolatry. It is an abortive search for meaning. In its early modern beginnings, racism was a justificatory device. It did not emerge as a faith. It arose as an ideological justification for the constellations of political and economic power which were expressed in colonialism and slavery. But gradually the idea of the superior race was heightened and deepened in meaning and value so that it pointed beyond the historical structures of relation, in which it emerged, to human existence itself. The alleged superior race became and now persists as a center of value and an object of devotion. Multitudes of men gain their sense of the "power of being" from their membership in the superior race. Accordingly, the most deprived white man, culturally and economically, is able to think of himself as "better'n any nigger."

The purpose of this book is to provide a Christian criticism of racism as a faith system in all of its facets and tendencies. By and large, Christians have failed to recognize racism as an idolatrous faith, even though it poses the problem of idolatry among Christians in a way that no other tendency does. Racism is especially problematical not only because of the peculiar nature of the racist faith, but because it is a "Trojan horse" within organized Christianity and Christian civic communities.

The procedure which is followed in this book is that of correlating the questions implied in the racist situation with the relevant answers of the Christian message. The search for meaning is first pursued from the side of racism. This is followed by the elaboration of Christian answers which are related to the situation. The use of the expression "the Christian . . ." in this book is done in full acknowledgment that a particular theological point of view is represented.

The Christian faith is brought into dialogue with racism for two reasons. First, I am convinced that Christian faith provides authentic answers to the questions which racism poses but to which racism is able to provide only false answers. Second, racism is a phenomenon of modern Christian civilization. By and large, the people who have been the racists of the modern world have also been Christians or the heirs of Christian civilization. Among large numbers of Christians, racism has been the other faith or one of the other faiths.

In scope, the analysis of racism is confined primarily to Negro-white relations in the United States. But a larger and supporting frame of reference is provided by drawing on pronouncements and interpretations of anti-Semitism and the anti-Caucasianism of the Black Muslims.

Certain terms are used which may require definition. The phrase, "Christian racist," will undoubtedly seem to many to contain a built-in contradiction. With those who must appeal to the words of Jesus, "You cannot serve God and mammon" (MATTHEW 6:24), I am obliged to agree. Authentic experience in the Christian community of faith issuing in total surrender to Christ cannot be conjoined with commitment to the idol god of race. But the term "Christian racist" is nevertheless used in this book in a loose way. It refers to historical and institutional fact only; it does not attempt to describe the heart. As a matter of fact, members of Christian churches do constitute and have constituted a large portion of the racists of the modern world. It is in this sense alone that I speak of "Christian racists." The term "polytheists" is also used to give such persons the benefit of the doubt, and to reflect an apparent obedience to multiple authority at the ultimate level.

The phrase "in-race" refers to the race of the speaker who makes the racist pronouncements or the actor who implements racist aims. The "out-race" is the ethnic group which is vilified, discriminated against, segregated, exterminated, or is to be exterminated in the great "eschatological event." The terms "aggressive racism" or "imperialistic racism" are used to describe white racism or racism in power. Black racism or Black Muslimism is referred to as "counter-racism" because it arises as a racist answer to white "imperialistic racism."

Racism has the character of faith in both its imperialistic and counter-racist forms, but an important distinction between the two must be noted. Imperialistic racism is full-bodied. It can walk on its feet and strike with its fists because its spirit permeates the institutions of power. A race as such lacks centeredness. The racist faith must therefore find its life through the use of political, military, economic, and cultural institutions. White men control the political, military, economic, and cultural institutions. Black men do not. Racism among the former is accordingly imperialistic and aggressive. They are able to project and implement concrete programs of political action while the Black Muslims must substitute eschatology for political action. Black Muslimism is racism out of power.

This difference is important to the analysis found in this book. The form of racism is a naturalistic ontology, but its vital principle is the will to power expressed in a political plan of action. Since Black Muslimism lacks power, it is not full-bodied racism. It lacks feet to walk on and fists with which to strike. The spirit is present; the hope is compelling; but the will to power cannot find the institutions of power through which it can express itself. The result of this distinction for this book is the fact that Black Muslimism provides no illustrative material for the study of racism in its most important facet—the plan of political action.

CONTENTS

RACISM AND THE CHRISTIAN UNDERSTANDING OF MAN

CHAPTER I

The Nature of the Racist Faith

A. Racism—modern phenomenon

RACISM is a modern phenomenon. It is a product of modern world conditions. It is a system of meaning and value that could only have arisen out of the peculiar conjunction of modern ideas and values with the political, economic, and technological realities of colonialism and slavery. Various forms of groupism appeared on the stage of history prior to the modern period, but none of them was racist.[1] In the late 1880's, the French racist philosopher Vacher de Lapouge wrote, "I am convinced that in the next century millions will cut each other's throats because of one or two degrees more or less of cephalic index." [2] In this statement, Lapouge gave a strictly modern reason for the mutual slaughter of men.

It is often said that racism has been a perennial problem in human history. But those who make this claim employ the concept of race erroneously. They loosely identify the idea of race with tribal, territorial, national, religious, and cultural groups. It is true that ethnocentrism—the belief in the unique value and rightness of one's own group

[1] The Hindu caste system of India is frequently identified with the caste practices of modern racism because it maintains itself primarily by direct blood relationship. But the Indian caste order is not based on color or physical characteristics in the sense that its objective is "purity of blood." The aim of the caste order is to preserve the sacred style of life. Sacred duties and ritualistic requirements are correlated with status and rank, and the community is accordingly preserved.

[2] Quoted in Ruth Benedict, *Race: Science and Politics* (rev. ed.; New York, 1947), p. 3.

—is universal as well as perennial. But ethnocentrism does not always take the form of racism.

The ethnocentrism of primitive in-groups is sometimes cited to show that racism is characteristic of human groups at all times and under all conditions. Primitive in-groups do think of themselves as the elect. They do often call themselves "the human beings" or "the men" while denying out-groups a place in the human scheme. But such sentiments among primitive tribes are expressions of their experience rather than of racist feelings. Whatever is outside its own territory is as alien to a primitive tribe as if it were on another planet. The tribe that supports itself adequately in its isolation, asks nothing of any other group; lacking a sense of common cause, it regards that which it takes from other people as clear gain.

> Even where primitive tribes include many thousands of people and occupy large territories, the picture usually does not differ essentially; the "in-group"—the tribal unit within which benefits are shared and activities carried out in common and where I behave with a certain ethical restraint toward my neighbors—this in-group knows its worth and claims unique importance.
>
> Such a primitive in-group is not a race, not even a small local sub-race or breed. The smallest racial unit is usually split up into many mutually death dealing in-groups. Their antagonism is not racial but cultural. They do not keep their "blood" separate; each tribe may have made a practice of raiding for women in the other group, and their ancestry therefore may be traceable to the despised group almost in the same proportion as to their own vaunted one. Or recurrent peacemaking between them may be signalized by inter-marriage, or marriages may be consummated for economic and social advantages. These practices occur whether neighboring tribes are of one breed, or whether they belonged at some period to two which can be distinguished by different anthropomorphic measurements. The duty to keep the "blood" unmixed is a refinement based on so-called science.[3]

The line of demarcation between groups is racial when the in-group seeks to keep its "blood" pure, no matter what the cultural state of affairs may be and no matter where the lines of political jurisdiction may be located. Ethnocentrism is not racial when it is based on religion, culture, class, or shared memories and experience.

Aristotle, among the ancients, is appealed to most frequently by scholars who contend that ethnocentrism in its racist form is perennial.

[3] Benedict, *op. cit.*, pp. 100–101.

Aristotle did state his disbelief that neither the fair-skinned barbarians nor the Asian peoples could rise to the cultural level of the Greeks. But he based this judgment on the ground that their cultural attainments were in fact inferior to Hellenistic achievement. Since he was not advancing a racist argument, he did not consider the Hellenized Asians, whose cultural attainments were high, to be pertinent to the argument. People who were un-Hellenized he thought inferior, but Aristotle did not argue in any of his writings that Greek "blood" must be kept pure. His best-known pupil, Alexander the Great, advocated intermarriage; in the course of his conquests, ten thousand of his soldiers took Indian wives.

The immediate background of modern racial alienation is the religious intolerance of the Middle Ages. In medieval culture, group antipathy and conflict on religious grounds was accepted as normative. The first victims of religious intolerance were heretics and Jews. But as Christianity and Islam became increasingly embroiled in religious rivalry, with each succeeding crusade, intolerance increased between the two faiths. Throughout the Mediterranean area, Christians enslaved Moslems, and Moslems enslaved Christians. Both groups enslaved pagans, heretics, and Jews. For each religious community, the human race was divided into two groups—"we" and "they." "We" and "they" meant believers and unbelievers. The unbeliever was considered a fit subject for conquest and enslavement.

As European expansion overseas increased, the believer-unbeliever line of demarcation was applied to Africans. The dark-skinned natives were regarded as outside the human community because they were thought to be without religion, law, or morals. They were not outside the human community because their skin was dark or their noses broad. During this earliest period of exploration and colonization, good Catholics believed that heathen and barbarous nations were outside the pale of both spiritual and civil rights by reason of their infidelity. Thus heathen lands were legitimate areas of conquest.

While the late medieval and early modern Church granted the right of conquest and enslavement of the heathen, it nevertheless imposed a responsibility with that right. In the fifteenth century Nicholas V issued a papal bull authorizing the Portuguese "to attack, subject, and reduce to perpetual slavery the Saracens, pagans, and other enemies of Christ southward of Cape Bojador and Non, including all the coast of Guinea." [4] The condition attached to this authorization was that the captives must be converted to Christianity, and conversion must be

[4] Quoted in Ina Corinne Brown, *Race Relations in a Democracy* (New York, 1949), p. 41.

followed by manumission. About a century after the bull of Nicholas V, a memorial of the Archbishop of Valencia was issued to Philip III of Spain. This memorial reaffirms the "Christian justification for conquest and enslavement," but it also reflects a new motive. The memorial explicitly affirms the economic motive in addition to that of conversion to Christianity as a justification for slavery.

> . . . Your majesty may, without any scruple of conscience, make slaves of all the Moriscos and may put them into your own galleys or mines, or sell them to strangers. And as to their children they may be all sold at good rates here in Spain, which will be so far from being a punishment, that it will be a mercy to them; since by that means they will all become Christians. . . . By the holy execution of which piece of Justice, a great sum of money will flow into your majesty's treasury.[5]

Through the decades, the gradually improving technology of transportation and military equipment of the European made slavery and colonialism larger, more profitable, and more prestige-bearing operations. This change meant that the medieval Christian justification for slavery and conquest was becoming a burden and a handicap. Political and economic interests were making necessary a new basis for the division between in-group and out-group. The shift from the idea of religious superiority to racial superiority was gradual. It developed as an ideological justification for political and economic interests that were already established and were in process of being expanded. Under the medieval requirement, Christians were permitted to conquer heathens in "just" wars and to enslave them, but they were required to convert and manumit their victims after a period of time. As the techniques of human and natural exploitation became more effective, and the European nations competed for colonial power, the conversion and manumission of the slaves became a pattern of behavior contrary to the political and economic interests of the exploiters. Since men are never willing to justify their behavior on the simple claim that might makes right or that their conduct satisfies their interests and desires, a new justification for colonialism and slavery was necessary. A ready-made explanation was at hand. The conquered and enslaved people were dark-skinned. The conquerors were white. Since the white people possessed a superior economic and military technology and were therefore able to conquer and enslave the people of color, it was a simple matter to explain the superiority of the cultural apparatus in terms

[5] *Ibid.*, p. 42.

of a superior human endowment. In other words, the exploiters read from right to left—from a cultural effect to a natural or congenital cause. Thus modern racism emerged as a sort of afterthought, a by-product of the ideological justification of European political and economic power arrangements over colored peoples—the justification of a set of advantages that medieval religious sanctions could no longer sustain.

For this reason, and because racial hostility is most potently manifest on the political and economic planes, many observers mistakenly assume that racism is nothing more than a device by which political, economic, and cultural interests are defended and expanded. Although racism did have its beginnings in a particular constellation of political and economic events in the early modern world, it has developed into an independent phenomenon, possessing meaning and value in itself and giving character to all the institutions of some societies. The cultural phenomenon that made its appearance in modern history as a form of self-justification and a defense of political and economic interests eventually became a complete system of meaning, value, and loyalty.

The fact that racism exists alongside other faiths does not make it any less a faith. Rather, this fact is testimony to the reality of polytheism in the modern age. In its maturity, racism is not a mere ideology that a political demagogue may be expected to affirm or deny, depending upon the political situation in which he finds himself. Racism is a search for meaning. The devotee of the racist faith is as certainly seeking self-identity in his acts of self-exaltation and his self-deifying pronouncements as he is seeking to nullify the selfhood of members of out-races by acts of deprivation and words of vilification.

B. Human alienation purely and simply

It is this faith character of racism which makes it the final and complete form of human alienation. Racism is human alienation purely and simply; it is the prototype of all human alienation. It is the one form of human conflict that divides human beings as human beings. That which the racist glorifies in himself is his being. And that which he scorns and rejects in members of out-races is precisely their human being. Although the racist line of demarcation and hostility inevitably finds expression through the institutions of society, it is not primarily a cultural, political, or economic boundary. Rather, it is a boundary of estrangement in the order of human being as such.

Accordingly, the basic racist affirmation of superiority, on the one hand, and inferiority, on the other, is not an empirical generalization as is commonly supposed. Rather, it is an affirmation concerning the fundamental nature of human beings. It is a declaration of faith that is neither supported nor weakened by any objective body of fact. Racism is an expression of the will to believe. The fundamental racist affirmation is that the in-race is glorious and pure as to its being, and out-races are defective and depraved as to their being. Any statement the racist makes concerning the cultural and political achievement, or potential, of the in-race or the out-races is based on this prior judgment concerning human being.

The claim of the racist that he studies the facts of history and arrives inductively at his generalizations is contradicted by his consistently negative response to contrasting situations. For example, when the racist asserts that Negroes cannot learn to operate complicated machinery or that all Jews are dishonest, instances to the contrary do not disturb his confidence in the truth of these generalizations. His confidence is not disturbed because his assertions are not empirical generalizations. The "facts" which the racist claims to be reading from Negro and Jewish character and behavior are in reality "faith" facts. Declarations of faith do not need to be proved from evidences in the objective world of facts. They do not need to be proved because the devotee of a faith is convinced that his faith assertions are reflections of the fundamental order of reality.

Thus when the racist sees Negroes actually operating complicated machinery he dismisses the meaning of what he sees by pointing out that these particular Negroes are "different." He believes that the place of the Negro is fixed in the fundamental order of reality: his status is not a matter of the accidents of history. And when the racist sees Jews who are honest by every objectively discernible standard available, he is still convinced that Jews are dishonest because the honesty of the Jew is Jewish honesty. To the anti-Semitic consciousness, the honesty of the Jew is not the same as the honesty of the Christian or non-Jew. The honesty of the Jew inheres in the Jewish being. Even the virtue of the Jew is therefore vice because it is his—because it inheres in defective being.

The claim that racism is human alienation purely and simply may be clarified by comparing racial alienation with other forms of human conflict. All other forms of collective hostility are expressions of conflict over some value or interest that exists *between* men. Human groups contend with each other because they cannot agree on the appropriate relationship each has to some value or values. For example, capital and labor struggle over the definition of their respective shares in the distribution of income from a product or a service. They also contend over their respective rights to power of decision in certain areas of economic process. The nations compete and contend against each other for land, minerals, markets, spheres of influence, and political hegemony. Organized religious bodies struggle with each other over the issues of who possesses the truth, of the proper means for its communication, and of the right to propagate it. Racial alienation stands alone among the forms of human conflict as the one form of collective hostility founded in the question of human being as such. A particular conflict among races may involve political or economic interests, but it is not the political or economic interests that make the conflict racial. The conflict is racial because of the racist faith present in the society involved. Numerous political and economic conflicts occur in one and the same society, but they have a racial character only when two or more racially related groups of that society are in contention. Furthermore, racial antipathy exists and persists in the hearts of men who have no contact whatsoever with the objects of their hostility. A popular saying in many suburbs and small towns of America is, "We do not have the problem because we do not have any of them here." The damaging nature of this claim to the very people who utter it is completely overlooked. It means that if any of *them* do show up, we are ready spiritually and politically to send them reeling back where they came from.

C. Christian racism implies a pejorative judgment concerning the action of God

Since racism assumes some segments of humanity to be defective in essential being, and since for Christians all being is from the hand of God, racism alone among the idolatries calls into question the divine creative action. The central claim of the racist is fundamentally a proposition concerning the nature of creation and the action of God rather than a doctrine concerning the nature of man. By implication, one part of the primary racist affirmation is the idea that God has made a creative error in bringing out-races into being. For Christians, the only possible theological alternative to the implication that God has made a creative error is the doctrine that out-races are the victims of a double fall. If the doctrine of the Demiurge had triumphed in Christianity, a third theological ground for explaining the existence of out-races would be available. But in the Gnostic controversies of the early Church the concept of the Demiurge was relegated to the limbo of heresy. In accounting for the origin of out-races, the Black Muslims enjoy a decided advantage over Christian racists. The creation mythology of the Black Muslims contains a Demiurge as the creator of the white man.

While Christian racists never appeal to the notion of the Demiurge to account for the nature of the existence of out-races, the doctrine of a second fall is explicitly enunciated in some naïve and obscurantist circles. The usual form of this theological proposition is the assertion that God himself has condemned Negroes to be "the hewers of the wood and drawers of the water now henceforth and forever" under the curse of Ham. A variation of the doctrine is the notion that Negroes are the descendants of Cain's union with an ape whom Cain, the first criminal, saw fit to marry "in the land of Nod." [6] This means that while the Negro shares the universal condemnation of the human race in Adam, he also bears the added condemnation of God in a special, racial fall. Since no promise of renewal and redemption is ever correlated with this second, special, racial fall, the Negro is a permanent victim of history and ultimately without hope. Whether the defectiveness in the humanity of out-races be an implication of the nature of creation or an explicit affirmation concerning a special, racial fall, the conclusion cannot be avoided that the action of God is the primary point of reference for Christian racists.

D. The faith character of racism

As a doctrine concerning the fundamental nature of human beings and a way of life elaborated on that doctrine, racism is a faith. H. Richard Niebuhr defines faith as "trust in that which gives value to the self," on the one hand; and on the other, "it is loyalty to what the self values." [7] It is in this sense that we speak of the racist faith.

In the experience of faith, the devotee has a double relation to the

[6] The idea of a racial fall is also ascribed to the Jews. It is the view, held by some Christians, that since the Jews are the chosen people, God has punished them and will continue to punish them until they acknowledge the Messiah. Thus the persecutions of Jews by Christians are preordained.

[7] H. Richard Niebuhr, *Radical Monotheism and Western Culture* (New York, 1960), p. 16.

object of faith. He trusts in it as the source of his personal value, and at the same time he is loyal to the object of his faith for the value it possesses independent of himself. Niebuhr illustrates this double relation in the life of the patriot whose faith is nationalism. The experience of the racist corresponds to that of the patriot, with the difference that the racist deifies his own being rather than an objective historic structure. The racist relies on the race as the source of his personal value. His life has meaning and worth because it is a part of the racial context. It fits into and merges with a valuable whole, the race. As the value-center, the race is the source of value, and it is at the same time the object of value. No questions can be raised about the rightness or wrongness of the race; it is the value-center which throws light on all other value. Criminals, degenerates, and even enemies have worth and goodness if they are members of the in-race. They have a goodness and worth which is not found in the most noble character of members of out-races, for goodness and worth are only secondarily qualities of behavior and character. Primarily they are qualities of being. Goodness and worth inhere in being that is worthy. If noble character inheres in a racially defective being, that person of noble character is nonetheless depraved, for the nobility he has achieved inheres in his unalterably corrupt humanity.

Therefore racism as a faith is a form of idolatry, for it elevates a human factor to the level of the ultimate. The god of racism is the race, the ultimate center of value. "What does it mean to have a god, or what is God?" Martin Luther inquires. Proceeding to answer his own question, Luther says, "trust and faith of the heart alone make both God and idol. . . . For the two, faith and God, hold close together. Whatever then thy heart clings to . . . and relies upon, this is properly thy God." [8] For the racist, race is the final point of reference for decision and action, the foundation upon which he organizes his private life, public institutions and public policy, and even his religious institutions. When men elevate any human or historical factor to so great a height that it has the power to give substance and direction to all cultural institutions, no matter what the *raison d'être*, that human or historical factor has become a god.

When the racist is also a Christian, which is often the case in America, he is frequently a polytheist. Historically, in polytheistic faiths, various gods have controlled various spheres of authority. Thus a Christian racist may think he lives under the requirements of the God of biblical faith in most areas of his life, but whenever matters of race

[8] Quoted in H. Richard Niebuhr, *op. cit.*, p. 119.

impinge on his life, in every area so affected, the idol of race determines his attitude, decision, and action.

Polytheistic faith has been nowhere more evident than in that sizable group of Christians who take the position that racial traditions and practices in America are in no sense a religious matter. These people assert that the whole field of race relations is an area with which religion has nothing to do. When pressed for a positive statement of the matter, they say that segregationist racial practices are merely amoral expressions of private preference. They completely overlook the fact that race relations are structured as a system which is not only enforced by the social mores but by institutional policy over all the country, and in some sections of the country, by law and public policy as well. The judgment that race relations involve amoral forms of behavior means in effect that interracial attitudes and practices are beyond the reach of Christian moral ideas and norms. The presence of polytheism among the adherents of the greatest monotheistic religion is not shocking in view of the insights of that very religion concerning original sin. The Old Testament provides ample historical evidence of man's continuous effort to restrict the Covenant of the Lord so that he may pursue certain interests and values as he sees fit. The prophetic tradition makes it equally clear that the only alternative to the worship of and obedience to the Lord God Jehovah is devotion to the Baals of the Canaanites.

It is an anomaly that morally concerned Christian leaders have rarely understood racism for what it really is. For a long time racist ideas and practices were viewed by morally sensitive Christians as nothing more than expressions of cultural lag and as products of ignorance. Since racial hostility is one of the forms of human conflict, many Christians have sought to understand racism wholly in terms of political, economic, and cultural factors. They have not seen the faith character of racist devotion and commitment, nor that racial antipathy is conflict in the order of humanity. A probable explanation of this peculiar state of affairs is that modern Christianity and Christian civilization have domesticated racism so thoroughly that most Christians stand too close to assess it properly.

E. The meaning of racism

The faith character of racism may be fully disclosed by an analysis of its various facets. In her *Race: Science and Politics*, Ruth Benedict defines racism as

> the dogma that one ethnic group is condemned by Nature to hereditary inferiority and another group is destined to hereditary superiority. It is the dogma that the hope of civilization depends upon eliminating some races and keeping others pure. It is the dogma that one race has carried progress throughout human history and can alone ensure future progress.[9]

From this definition, it may be seen first of all that racism is a form of naturalism. Man owes his existence to nature and nature controls his destiny. Nature has condemned inferior races and blessed the superior race. This means that the fundamental thing about a man is his body, specifically his genetic structure. Mental and spiritual qualities depend upon the natural quality, and are, in fact, but expressions of it.

This naturalistic view of man is diametrically opposed to the biblical doctrine of the creation of man in the image of God; it is also opposed to the main tendencies in the development of Western philosophy. One of the great anomalies of our time is the fact that the racist ideology has taken so firm a grasp upon the heirs of both traditions, and has emerged in the modern world which is precisely that world wherein philosophy and theology broke their esoteric bonds, and became widely available, at least in their main ideas, through popular education.

It must be observed that not all people who understand man naturalistically in the context of race relations subscribe to the naturalistic doctrine in general. Some Christians would be horrified to discover that they really believe in a naturalistic view of man when race relations call for decision and action. If told that this is the case, they will vigorously deny it. Many of them are quite orthodox in their theology and even literalistic in their approach to the Bible. In the abstract, they constantly repeat the phrase that God has created all men in His own image. In the abstract, they believe that the essence of man is spirit. But when they actually view the races in relation to each other, or make social and political decisions concerning race, they bring judgments to bear upon the situation which clearly indicate their belief that the races are poles apart in the order of humanity and that the ground of the great human differences lies in the genes.

The fact that racist claims are affirmations concerning the fundamental nature of humanity, rather than empirical generalizations as they are popularly thought to be, may be made more evident by a few illustrations. During the last war, General J. L. DeWitt was in charge

[9] Benedict, *op. cit.*, p. 98.

of the evacuation of naturalized Japanese from California. General DeWitt made the following statement concerning Japanese Americans: "A Jap's a Jap. . . . It makes no difference whether he is an American citizen or not. . . . I don't want any of them here. . . . They are a dangerous element. . . . There is no way to determine their loyalty." [10] In another statement, General DeWitt made it unqualifiedly clear that the element which he regarded as evil within the Japanese character is incorrigible because it is rooted in the genetic structure. "The Japanese race is an enemy race and while many second and third generation Japanese born on United States soil, possessed of United States citizenship, have been 'Americanized' the racial strains are undiluted." [11]

The study of racial stereotypes shows conclusively that out-races are hated and regarded as threats even when the traits that are ascribed to them are admirable and normally regarded as virtues. Americans, like all people, admire intelligence, industry, skill, and sobriety. But when these traits appear in a Negro, he may be condemned rather than admired. The Negro who manifests these virtues is charged with being "uppity" and with having "gotten out of his place." This charge is made right along with the claim that Negroes get nowhere because they are lazy, stupid, slovenly, unambitious, and intemperate. Frequently, Jews and Japanese find themselves isolated and threatened precisely because of their virtues. In 1921 Dr. Benjamin I. Wheeler, president emeritus of the State University of California, said of the Japanese-Americans, "Their good taste, their persistent industry, their excellent qualities and their virtues render their presence amongst us a pitiful danger." [12] This queer response to a people because of their virtue illustrates that the hostility toward and rejection of out-races is not based on their culture and behavior. Racists condemn Japanese-Americans because they believe that they are defective as human beings. Since their virtues must inhere in a supposedly corrupt ground, even their virtues are seen as vices.

Writing in the *London Daily Chronicle* many years ago on the inconsistency of stereotypes ascribed to the Jew, Lloyd George con-

[10] U.S. Army, Western Defense Command and Fourth Army, Final Report, Japanese Evacuation from the West Coast, 1942 (Washington, D.C., Government Printing Office, 1943), p. 34; quoted in Charles Abrams, *Forbidden Neighbors* (New York, 1955), p. 41. [11] *Ibid.*

[12] Abrams, *op. cit.*, p. 39; quoting Colonel John P. Irish, "The Japanese Issue in California," *The Annals of the American Academy of Political and Social Science*, XCIII (January, 1921), p. 75.

cluded that the Jew is believed to be bad, no matter what he is or does. He is bad because he is a Jew.

Similarly, in all opposition to the plan of open occupancy in housing, it is the potential *presence* of a Negro, a Jew, an Oriental, in a neighborhood which evokes hostility and often causes panic-selling. It is not the potential *behavior* of the minority group member. Almost no one bothers to inquire about his character, reputation, or cultural traits. His potential presence in the neighborhood is not that of an individual. To the racist, he lacks individuality. He is an instance of a depraved type. Even if his character and ideals are lofty, they are his and are therefore vices. They are vices because only vice can inhere in depraved being. Any Negro, no matter what his personal qualifications are, is believed to blight a neighborhood by simply being there.

In 1943 the National Association of Real Estate Boards issued a supplementary brochure to its official code entitled, "Fundamentals of Real Estate Practice." In this brochure a Negro, even as a man of achievement and high aspiration, is grouped with immoral and shady characters as an undesirable:

> The prospective buyer might be a bootlegger who would cause considerable annoyance to his neighbors, a madam who had a number of call girls on her string, a gangster, who wants a screen for his activities by living in a better neighborhood, a colored man of means who was giving his children a college education and thought they were entitled to live among whites. . . . No matter what the motive or character of the would-be purchaser, if the deal would instigate a form of blight, then certainly the well-meaning broker must work against its consummation.[13]

It is clear from the directive contained in this brochure that real estate men are being advised that Negroness in itself is corrupt and therefore produces blight in a neighborhood. The one reference to the achievement of the colored man is that he is a man of means, a fact that brings honor and respect to white Americans. The one reference to his behavior is that he is giving his children a college education, a commendable parental act when divorced from the concept of "the Negro's place." And the one reference to the aspirations of the colored man is that he thought his children were entitled to live among whites. Translated into the experience of a white person, this would simply be

[13] *Ibid.*, p. 156; quoted in *Equality of Opportunity in Housing* (New York: National Community Relations Advisory Council, June, 1952), p. 15.

expressed as the legitimate desire to live in a better neighborhood and to share the benefits that it offered. In short, all the references to the character and behavior of the colored man would be considered praiseworthy in a white man. But with all these personal assets, the Negro's presence "would instigate a form of blight." The conclusion cannot be escaped that it is his being that is alleged to be corrupt. It is his Negroness. It is precisely that which God has given him.

Racially exclusive property owners, supported by real estate men, claim ad nauseum that they are trying to maintain "standards of culture, congeniality, and happiness." But there is much evidence that racial homogeneity is exalted above all moral and cultural considerations. The disclosure that professional hoodlums and racketeers of various kinds are in fact located in the "best neighborhoods" is the most telling evidence against the idealistic claims of exclusivistic property owners and real estate men. Gangsterism, hoodlumism, and prostitution among white persons are not thought by the racist to be as deeply defective as being born a member of an out-race. The deepest of all corruptions in the racist mind is the being of members of out-races.

The second feature of racism, in our definition, is that it is a plan of political action. "It is the dogma that the hope of civilization depends upon eliminating some races and keeping others pure." [14] The elimination of some races has not, for the most part, been carried to its logical limit in Western history. The reduction of life by means of deprivation has usually been a substitute for the elimination of races. Accordingly, the chief political plan of the racists has been segregation, involving as it does, subordination, suppression, isolation, and deprivation. But despite the prevailing practice of segregation, the logic of racism is genocide. The logic of racism is genocide because that which is wrong with an out-race is its fundamental being. The alleged evil in an out-race does not lie in historical functions, events, and relationships. It lies in the human nature of the out-race. For the racist, an out-race is not fundamentally a sociological problem; an out-race is a problem in the order of human being. It is a sociological problem only for the deeper reason that it is a human problem. The segregation and subordination of a people because they are defective in being as such is obviously an inadequate handling of the situation. The problem of defective humanity cannot be resolved by segregation and quarantine; it requires the final solution. The final solution is extermination. If only segregation and quarantine are employed, the racist must continuously

[14] Benedict, *op. cit.*, p. 98.

fear that the defectiveness of the out-race will infiltrate his own race through intermarriage. The elimination of the out-race is the logical and final solution of the problem. Adolf Hitler and his Nazi associates were quite logical in their racial program within the premises of their racist faith. When an American racist says, "All niggers ought to be dead," he is speaking a philosophical mouthful. He is voicing the logic of his philosophy, which is to will the death of the Negro. Racism is total hate. It is literally to "hate the guts" of the other race, for it is hatred of the created being of the other.

Perhaps many people who have racism in their hearts have never been able to face up to the logical requirements of their racist god because they are trying to open their hearts to Christ also. But when they shall have found the freedom to look deeply within, they will discover what was really in their hearts. They will know that their commitment was to a god who required more of them than the practice of the customary subordinations, deprivations, and spatial exclusions of out-races. If a racist is true to his faith, it is not enough that he exclude out-races from jobs, neighborhoods, clubs, schools, or churches. The racist faith demands the exclusion of out-races from existence. Out-races must be excluded from existence because it *is* their existence which is alleged to be corrupt. To the racist, the existence of out-races is not mere estrangement from the in-race; it is not mere alienation; it is depravity of being. Therefore the proposition in our definition of racism that it "is the dogma that the hope of civilization depends upon eliminating some races and keeping others pure" is a correct judgment of the matter.

We have referred to segregation as the principal plan of political action of the racist faith. The use of the phrase "political plan of action" may be misconstrued. This phrase does not mean, as it may seem, the mere application of the faith. The plan of political action is inherent to the faith. It is as fundamental to the racist faith as is the naturalistic doctrine of man. Racism is inherently an oppressive and brutal system. It is inherently the will to power. The will to reduce the life of the other is the inevitable correlate of the exaltation and glorification of the self. And since, in the racist consciousness, the other race is defective in being as such, it is his being which must be reduced and eliminated. A naturalistic view of man is the philosophic formulation of racism, but the political plan of action is its vital impulse.

The idea that segregation is a religion is ably supported by James Sellars in his book *The South and Christian Ethics*.[15] The position ad-

[15] James Sellars, *The South and Christian Ethics* (New York, 1962).

vanced here is basically in agreement with that of Sellars. A minor difference lies in the fact that Sellars regards segregation as a religion, while we are asserting that segregation is a facet of the larger faith of racism. Segregation is racism's vital impulse in that it has historically been the principal plan of political action.

Two letters to the *Nashville Banner*, stating the religious case for segregation, are cited and interpreted by Sellars. From the substance of these letters, the conclusion may be drawn that the writers were Christian racists. One of them was a man from Columbia, Tennessee, who wrote: "Segregation is not a religious issue and never was. God is the author of segregation. He is a God of segregation." [16] Sellars points out that the writer of the letter affirms both that segregation is not religious, and yet ordained of God. Obviously, it cannot be both. The resolution of this contradiction is as follows:

> The author's meaning, I think, is this: segregation is religious, all right, but it is not a religious issue. An issue is something you can argue about. Segregation, on the other hand, is so God-ordained, and therefore religious, that it is not a question.[17]

The other correspondent to the *Nashville Banner* states the religious case for segregation by placing the emphasis on the action of man—his being religious and doing the religious thing. "The country was equally religious before the unfortunate decision of the Supreme Court and its rulings have created no new religious law, regardless of the decision of some churchmen." [18] Sellars concludes that in both letters the effort is to affirm that segregation is theologically self-evident. It is beyond discussion and must be accepted in the same way that the dogmas of the Christian faith are accepted.

The third element in our definition of racism is that it is a philosophy of history. It is the dogma that one race has carried progress throughout human history and alone can ensure future progress. We have already pointed out that racism is a search for meaning. As a philosophy of history, racist dogma purports to interpret the meaning of the whole human historical process. The meaning of human existence is quite simple to the racist consciousness. It is found in the cultural expressions of the superior race, when these expressions issue directly from the uncontaminated "racial instincts" of that race.

As a philosophy of history, the similarity between racism and communism is striking. While communism teaches that the whole cultural

[16] *Ibid.*, p. 115. [17] *Ibid.*, p. 116. [18] *Ibid.*

superstructure rests on the economic substructure, racism teaches that the whole cultural superstructure rests on the genetic substructure. While communism teaches that the final solution of the problem of history awaits the triumph of the proletariat and the ushering in of the classless society by the proletariat, racism teaches that the final solution of the problem of history awaits the realization of the Germanic ideal of superior race or the genetic renewal of man.

The first of these claims means that the quality of the superior race is the absolute determinant of history, and that quality is biological. The essence of man is his genetic structure. This doctrine has been repeated by numerous racist philosophers and is found among many laymen in the United States, at times in the form of a vulgarized Darwinism. The central ideas of this doctrine are the notions that culture is transmitted through the genes and that the mechanism of inheritance operates through races rather than families.

The second claim in the racist philosophy of history, that having to do with destiny, elevates the alleged superior race to the status of lords rather than bearers of history. Meaningful history is found exclusively in the decisions and deeds of the superior race. Meaningful history is identical with racial history. There is no center of meaning above history which may be drawn upon. There is no final realization after a period of growth in virtue. Meaning in history emerges from below, from nature, from the genes. History is fulfilled when the racial strains of the superior race are given unqualified cultural expression. This simple biological interpretation enables the racist philosopher to assume that history has actually been fulfilled from time to time, only to be corrupted eventually by race mixture.

CHAPTER II

Self-Understanding and Understanding of the Other

A. Knowledge of the self in antithetical relation to the other

THE racist consciousness operates in what Martin Buber has called "the World of It." [1] The World of It is the world of objects and things. In this world there is a single center of consciousness. This single subject, the "I," experiences, arranges, and appropriates. It does not enter into relationship with other, different beings. It experiences human beings racially different from itself only as "the other," as antithetical to the self in the order of humanity. The "I" self "knows" itself as pure being while it "knows" the other as depraved being. The "I" self does not enter into communion with the other, for the other is not known as "Thou." The other is first, last, and always "It." The other is an object to be used, manipulated, or eliminated. But since the other in fact belongs to the order of human being, and not merely to the animal kingdom, the relation of the self to the other is on a different plane than the relation of the self to the worlds of animality and nature. The self is aware that the other is in some sense a center of consciousness. The fact that the other in some way belongs on the same plane with the self will not down. The radical contrast between the self and the other can therefore be expressed only in polar terms. The racist consciousness knows itself in contrast, in polarity with and opposition to the racially contemptible object. This means that in the

[1] Martin Buber, *I and Thou*, trans. Ronald Gregor Smith (New York, 1937).

racial context, the racist cannot know himself until he first knows the other. The racist is completely dependent upon the antithetical correlation. When the other is properly experienced, appropriated, and arranged, the racist consciousness can know itself as the other pole in a structure of human contrasts.

The idea that the Negro appears in the anti-Negro consciousness as a contrast conception was ably presented by Lewis Copeland about a generation ago, but very little has been made of this notion in the literature of race relations. Copeland found the social opposition between Negroes and whites so sharp as to give rise to a conceptual dichotomy "somewhat analogous to that between God and the devil in popular religion." [2] And just as in popular religion the contrast between God and the devil introduces a dichotomy which is conceived as running through the whole universe, dividing both the natural world and the social order, the counterconcepts of the racist consciousness "form the basis for the interpretation of human nature and society." [3]

The idea of the contrast conception as a basic constituent of the racist self-consciousness seems to have originated with Erich Voegelin. In his *Rasse und Staat*, Voegelin develops the thesis that Judaism in Christian Germany is a counterconception. Likewise, Jean-Paul Sartre, writing on French anti-Semitism,[4] designates the Jew as a contrast conception. When the anti-Semite speaks of Jewish avarice, says Sartre, he means there is a "Jewish" avarice, an avarice determined by that synthetic whole, the Jewish person. This avarice is different from Christian avarice. It is not the universal, human trait of avarice, but an avarice which emerges from a unique synthesis, the Jewish being.

In popular thought in America, black and white have become conceptual opposites.

> The black man and his appurtenances stand at the antithesis of the character and properties of the white man. The conception makes of the Negro a counter-race. The black race serves as a foil for the white race, by which the character of the latter is made all the more impressive.[5]

The antipodal positions of the two races are often verbalized in the phrase "the opposite race." In its fullest meaning, the word "opposite"

[2] Lewis C. Copeland, "The Negro as a Contrast Conception," in Edgar T. Thompson, ed., *Race Relations and the Race Problem* (Durham, N.C., 1939), p. 152. [3] *Ibid.*

[4] *Anti-Semite and Jew*, trans. George J. Becker (New York, 1960).

[5] Copeland, *op. cit.*, p. 153.

is a reference to more than the extremes of color. It suggests the two opposites of human being. An examination of the counter-racist consciousness discloses the same element. Eric Lincoln writes:

> To a great extent the Muslims define their movement by negative contrast to their most important audiences; Negroes, Jews, the orthodox Moslems in America and the hated whites. They assert their strength and purity by castigating the weakness and depravity they claim to see among these strangers.[6]

To the Black Muslim, knowledge of the self has its corollary in "the truth about the white man." [7] The Black Muslim therefore cannot "know" himself until he first "knows" the white man. Knowledge of "the truth about the white man" produces knowledge of the self as the opposite in the order of human being.

While physical traits are assumed to be the basis of the racial distinction, social traits are correlated with them. "The essence of the racial contrast appears to be a moral antithesis which tends to be projected through all social relations." [8] In his book, *The Negro as Beast,* Charles Carroll saw the contrast in such extreme terms that the idea of polar opposites proved to be inadequate. Nothing less than the nature of God the Creator is sufficient to explain the difference between the black and the white races. Carroll wrote that the white and the Negro races "present the strongest contrast to each other in their physical and mental characters" and in their mode of life. From this he drew the conclusion that "since God created man in his own image, and God is not a Negro, then the Negro is not human but a beast." [9]

Numerous pejorative terms are employed to describe the Negro in the moral antithesis. He is alleged to be subhuman in temperament, lacking in emotional control and restraint, brutish and vulgar by nature, promiscuous as an animal, lacking in the capacity for continuous affection and mental concentration, lacking in the capacity for lasting, sacrificial friendship or love, and possessing only a sensual love. The Negro mother allegedly neglects even her offspring. One informant attributed the immorality of the Southern white man to the seductive powers of the Negro woman.

> The Negro has degraded Southern morality. We cannot have any moral standards with so many free and easy Negro women

[6] Eric Lincoln, *The Black Muslims in America* (Boston, 1961), p. 135.

[7] *Ibid.*, p. 190. [8] Copeland, *op. cit.*, pp. 155–156.

[9] *Ibid.*, pp. 156–157.

> running loose. Most every Negro wench is a prostitute. I don't call it seduction by white men, for what really happens is the Negro women seduce the white men. Sex is the basis of the whole problem.[10]

The counter-racist description of the white man in the moral antithesis matches the vitriolic quality of the aggressive racist description of the black man. Typical of the Black Muslim image of the white man is the following observation by Elijah Muhammed in an issue of his regular newspaper column:

> The human beast—the serpent, the dragon, the devil, and Satan —all mean one and the same: the people or race known as the white or Caucasian race, sometimes called the European race. They are the great universal deceivers of non-white people, the greatest murderers . . . whoever lived or ever will live on our planet earth.[11]

The moral antithesis in terms of which the racist consciousness understands the self and the other is an important element in the religious dimension of racism. The interracial experience to the racist involves elements of emotive power beyond any conscious and deliberate choice on the part of the racist agent. In regard to the significance of the moral distinction, Copeland concludes: "Moral distinctions are the final rationalizations of racial contrasts, for through these collective representations the counter ideas of race are reduced to feelings and sentiments; they become emotive in nature." [12] More important than anything else is that the racial difference is felt to make a difference of polar proportions.

Since the color of bodies has a moral connotation for the racist consciousness, it is a simple matter for that consciousness to project this connotation throughout the social order, and to attach it to objects and acts. Accordingly, that which is good is white and that which is bad is black. God himself is white: the devil is black. Racial terms, in the racist world of thought, come to symbolize values and expectations in general. If things do not measure up to expectations, they are "nigger" or "niggerish." Copeland cites such examples as a bad bridge, which is called a "nigger bridge," or an unattractive dog, which is "just an ol' cur like you'd see round any nigger house." [13] Many instances in which the racial term is transferred to animals, plants, objects, etc., are

[10] *Ibid.*, p. 158.

[11] Elijah Muhammed, "Mr. Muhammed Speaks," *The Pittsburgh Courier*, December 13, 1958, p. 14.

[12] Copeland, *op. cit.*, p. 158.

[13] *Ibid.*, p. 159.

cited in Murray's *New English Dictionary*. "Thus hard coconut shells are called 'Negro-skulls.' . . . Coarse cloth is 'Negro-cloth,' and rank cheap grades of black tobacco are called 'niggerhead twist.'" [14] A bad game of bridge is referred to as "nigger" bridge, inefficient lazy methods of work are designated as "niggerish." To "nigger-out" signifies "to exhaust the land." Thus racial beliefs create two social orders, two moral universes, dichotomies in nature and in artifacts. Not only do the two races belong to two social universes but objects and acts are relegated to their respective Negro and white spheres.

Racial values find their fullest symbolic expression in the moral antithesis which is ascribed to white and black females. The white woman is the most conspicuous symbol of racial values. "The loveliest and purest of God's creatures, the nearest thing to an angelic being that treads this terrestrial ball, is a well-bred, cultured Southern white woman or her blue-eyed, golden-haired little girl." [15] On the contrary, the Negro woman stands as the symbol of degradation. The term frequently used to designate her is "wench."

The social effect of the ideological dichotomy is universal segregation. The races are to be separated in every aspect of their existence. It is assumed that every system of belief and loyalty of which the white man is a part excludes the Negro because they are polar opposites.

> A Negro salesman called on a white businessman after his concern had written for an appointment. When he appeared with his samples, he was ordered out of the store. "You go back and tell your company that I'm a Democrat, a Methodist, and a Southerner, and I don't want any Negro coming around my place." [16]

The manager had obviously expected the salesman to be white and was prepared to give him the conventional reception. But when a Negro appeared, he was rejected, not merely in the business world, but on the strength of several other systems of belief and loyalty. The contrast conception of race is so basic and so strong that it is determinative of all systems of belief and value when these relate to race relations. The Negro is an alien in the whole of the white man's universe, whether the area of concern be business, politics, region, or religion. He is not a part of any "public" to which the white man belongs. Thus, when it is announced that "the public is invited," no Negroes are expected be-

[14] *Ibid.*, p. 160.

[15] Tom Brady, *Black Monday;* quoted by James Graham Cook in *The Segregationists* (New York, 1962), p. 18.

[16] Copeland, *op. cit.*, pp. 165–166.

cause they are not thought of as a part of "the public." Even the announcement on a church bulletin reading "All Are Welcome" usually does not refer to Negroes because the inclusiveness of the word "all" falls short of embracing them. Aggressive racism assigns two statuses to the Negro in America. First, the Negro exists as an isolated and subordinated man. Second, in some contexts, he "exists" as a nonentity.

A social and political system established on these ideas requires that the Negro never for a moment forget "his place" in society. If he does, the whole weight of the powers and sanctions of society are brought down upon him. It is assumed that every system of meaning and value requires that he stay in "his place." On the other hand, "to mistake a white man for a Negro is a heinous offense, and according to court decisions, does violence to the feelings of persons. To refer to a white man as a 'nigger lover' is the most damning of epithets." [17]

The value and use of the racial dichotomy in the racist system is summarized as follows:

> The traditional racial ideology has thus made of the black man a devil, a bogey-man, the epitome of evil and badness. He is a foil that sets off the white social values, lending to them an increased splendor. The use to which the black race is put is cryptically suggested by the story of the little girl who cried because the Negroes were leaving. When asked why she was crying, she replied, "when the Negroes are all gone there won't be anybody to be better than." [18]

The notion of the "opposite race" has already been referred to as the verbal expression of the fundamental contrast between the races in the racist consciousness. But this is not the only meaning of the phrase. The idea of the "opposite race" is also freighted with historical meaning. The black race is believed to be the perennial enemy of the white race, against whom all whites must unite. "Opposite race" thus means "race in opposition." Since the dichotomy between the races is made a moral one, the contrast between them is historical and dynamic as well as fundamental. The struggle against the black man therefore takes on the character of moral compulsion. It is a perennial call to political action. Thus it is said:

> We have to stand up for our kind. Wherever you see white and black they will never mix. The two are always at war with each

[17] *Ibid.*, p. 161. [18] *Ibid.*, p. 162.

other—and always will be. We white people have got to stand together or else be beaten down by the black man. . . . We just have to keep these Negroes in their place. When things get so bad that you cannot do it by talking to them, we have to get together to beat them down.[19]

By positing an enemy race, the racist ideology produces cohesion within white society. At this point, the ideology is a call to vigilance, and if need be, to attack. The Negro is pictured as a continuous threat, who becomes aggressive whenever the lines of restraint are slackened. Despite the fact that he is politically and economically weak, his behavior is described by the terms of power and aggression. He "takes" white men's jobs. He "invades" their residential neighborhoods. He constantly wishes to "force" himself "where he is not wanted." In politics, he is virtually an opposition party, which must be defeated.

Counter-racism also views the out-race as the "opposite race" historically as well as fundamentally. The basic claim of Elijah Muhammed is that the white man is "the human beast—the serpent, the dragon, the devil, and Satan" because he was so created. But the Messenger of Allah also stresses that white men have historically embodied the role of enemies of all "truth and righteousness and the enemies of those who seek the truth." According to the Muslim mythology, Allah has given the devils (white men) six thousand years to rule.[20] During this reign, the devils have

deceived the black nations of the earth, trapped and murdered them by hundreds of thousands, divided and put black against black, corrupted and committed fornication before your very eyes with your women . . . [and then made] you confess that you love them.[21]

Against the background of this history, Elijah Muhammed declares Caucasians to be the enemy race of black people and a people who cannot be trusted. The Caucasians are great deceivers. Their very nature, says Muhammed, is against friendship with black people, although they often fool the black people, making them believe that they are their sincere friends. The advice which is deemed appropriate to these

[19] *Ibid.*, p. 168.

[20] The allotted span ended in 1914. The white man is now ruling during the "years of grace," a 70-year period ending in 1984. Lincoln, *op. cit.*, p. 77.

[21] Elijah Muhammed, *op. cit.*, p. 14.

claims is: "Do not 'sweetheart' with white people, your open enemies, for their 'sweethearting' with you is not sincere." [22]

B. The stereotype

The articles of faith of the racist ideology are called stereotypes. The racial stereotype embodies the tradition of hostility toward out-races, and, accordingly, primarily aims to describe out-races. But the in-race inevitably stereotypes itself, since it glorifies iself, as the contrast of every expression of depravity in out-races. Gordon W. Allport defines the stereotype as "an exaggerated belief associated with a category. Its function is to justify (rationalize) our conduct in relation to that category." [23] The category is "Negro," "Jew," "Mexican," etc. Each of these categories may be held in mind in a neutral, factual, and nonevaluative way. But when a statement is made concerning one of these categories in such a way as to give an exaggerated importance to a few characteristics, a stereotype has been uttered. A stereotype may be favorable or unfavorable. If it purports to describe the in-race, it is always favorable. If it purports to describe the out-race, it is always unfavorable. In either case, it works as a justificatory device and has the effect of oversimplifying perception and thinking.

Typification, applied to human beings, passes by that which makes the individual unique, unexchangeable, and irreplaceable. The typifier or stereotyper poses his own problem and sets out on his own purpose in the act of stereotyping.

It must be observed that stereotypes do contain elements of truth. But stereotypes do not aim to present the truth. They aim to present generalizations in such a way that categories will be accepted or rejected. The stereotype is a device which is used to persuade, not to inform. The elements of truth which are stated are therefore set in a compound of error, exaggeration, omission, and half-truth. An illustration of the mixture of truth with error in the stereotype is presented in the following statement:

> If we think of the Irish as more prone to alcoholism than, say, Jews, we are making a correct judgment in terms of probability.

[22] Elijah Muhammed, "Mr. Muhammed Speaks," *The Pittsburgh Courier*, August 9, 1958, p. 14.

[23] Gordon W. Allport, *The Nature of Prejudice* (Garden City, N.Y., 1958), p. 187.

> Yet if we say, "Jews don't drink," or "the Irish are whiskey soaked," we are manifestly exaggerating the facts, and building up an unjustified stereotype. We can distinguish between a valid generalization and a stereotype only if we have solid data concerning the existence of (the probability of) true differences.[24]

Probably the chief practical function of the stereotype in aggressive racism is its service in calling people to the action which produces the very results described by the stereotype. Stereotypes, of course, justify the existing power arrangements. They are always operative even when there is no need for their special proclamation. But stereotypes come alive and are repeated with evangelistic fervor when they describe a situation calling for present and immediate action. The stereotype used in this manner is called a self-fulfilling prophecy.

Robert K. Merton defines self-fulfilling prophecy as follows: "If men define situations as real, they are real in their consequences." [25] It is not necessary that situations actually be real. It is only necessary that they be defined as real, and that those who make the definitions have the power to actualize situations according to their definitions. Men do respond to the objective features of situations. But men do not merely respond to the objective features, and sometimes they do not respond primarily to them. Rather, the responses of men are often directed to the meaning which they have assigned to the situation. "And once they have assigned some meaning to the situation, their consequent behavior and some of the consequences of that behavior are determined by the ascribed meaning." [26] Merton says of self-fulfilling prophecy that it "is, in the beginning, a false definition of the situation evoking a new behavior which makes the originally false conception come true. The specious validity of the self-fulfilling prophecy perpetuates a reign of error." [27]

Merton illustrates how the exclusionist policies of labor unions against Negroes, justified in the first place by stereotypes, produced the very "facts" which constituted the original stereotypes. The union member assumes that his decision is based on the hard, cold facts of the situation. The Negro laborer has migrated from the nonindustrialized parts of the South. He lacks background in the traditions of trade unions and the practice of collective bargaining. He has always

[24] *Ibid.*, p. 188.

[25] Robert K. Merton, "A Social Psychological Factor," in Arnold M. Rose, ed., *Race Prejudice and Discrimination* (New York, 1951), p. 510.

[26] *Ibid.* [27] *Ibid.*, p. 512.

been the victim of a low standard of living. And since he readily accepts jobs at rates lower than the prevailing wages, he is a strikebreaker, a depressor of the wage scale, a scab. But to the labor unionist, the Negro is not merely an economic threat by history, he is an economic threat by nature. He is the opposite race. The unionist is caught in the vicious circle of his own self-fulfilling prophecies, and does not understand that he and others who share his pattern of thinking and acting have produced the very facts which he proclaims in the stereotype.

> For by defining the situation as one in which Negroes are held to be *incorrigibly* at odds with principles of unionism and by excluding Negroes from unions, he invited a series of consequences which indeed made it difficult if not impossible for many Negroes to avoid the role of scab. Out of work after World War I and kept out of unions, thousands of Negroes could not resist strikebound employers who held a door invitingly open upon a world of jobs from which they were otherwise excluded.[28]

All stereotyping is alike in form in that it is exaggerated generalization which passes beyond individual variations. But all stereotyping is not alike in use and effect. This distinction is often missed by people who are well meaning but detrimentally naïve in their understanding of racial stereotyping. Many Christian people vigorously defend the annual minstrel show in their churches and communities as harmless occasions of jollity and good fellowship. They deny that anyone has the slightest intention to disparage any group. Similarly, the same people defend racial jokes and stories as only a part of healthy and wholesome joviality. They point to the fact that stereotyping is universal and that there are all kinds of national, ethnic, and racial stories and jokes. What such persons fail to understand is the profound difference between stereotypes applied to in-groups and those applied to out-groups. One and the same trait may be ascribed to an in-group and an out-group, but with a profound difference in use and effect. For example, people of Scottish background are often the butt of stories which illustrate extreme frugality. Such stories are told in a spirit of levity and good feeling. But when a story of essentially the same content is told of a Jew, the trait is changed from "frugality" to "miserliness," and the point of the story becomes a call to renewed vigilance in dealing with Jews. The difference lies in the fact that aggressive racism has already marked off out-races as objects of hostility and control, and

[28] *Ibid.*, p. 513.

employs stereotypes as defenses of the status quo and political calls to action. The racial stereotype is a call to the continuance or intensification of existing structures of racial relationships. If the typifier has control over those typified, the spoken or written word of justification becomes effective in social and political institutions and policies. On the other hand, stereotypes ascribed to ethnic or nationality groups who belong to the in-group or to groups over whom the typifier has absolutely no control are politically ineffectual and are devoid even of political intent.

> The American way of life is not disturbed by the fact that foreigners identify it with the pattern presented by Hollywood films. Nor has the image won from the reading of French novels or comedies any influence on real French family life. If, however, the outsider [in the case in point, the aggressive racist] has the power to impose his system of relevances upon the individuals typified by him, and especially to enforce its institutionalization, then this fact will create various repercussions on the situation of the individuals typified against their wills.[29]

In short, when power is combined with racial hatred, the whole stereotypical system may become one of self-fulfilling prophecy. An illustration from the Negro's Southern past may be instructive in this connection.[30] Until recently the belief was held almost universally that the Negro could not learn to operate complicated machinery. This belief was conjoined with contemptuous attitudes toward the Negro and the will to subordinate him. Accordingly, the Negro was denied the right of technical education. This denial created a situation in which there were no Negroes operating complicated machinery. This situation in turn "proved" the correctness of the stereotype.

It appears that many racists sincerely believe that their generalizations are empirical. They constantly appeal to what they call the facts. But when pressed, racists quickly reveal that they are making affirmations that do not need to be supported by facts. They are "felt in the blood," and are expressions of a faith commitment. It is this faith quality of racism which enables the devotee equally to condemn out-races for contradictory sets of traits, even though one may be the same set

[29] Alfred Schutz, "Equality and the Meaning Structure of the World," in Lyman Bryson *et al.*, eds., *Aspects of Human Equality* (New York, 1956), pp. 63–64.

[30] The intention here is not to suggest that such ideas and behavior are all in the past but to recognize the dawning of a new day.

of traits which the racist praises in his own race. Negroes are called inferior because they are judged to be lazy, devoid of ambition, uninhibited, loud, dirty, superstitious, etc. But Jews and Japanese are regarded as threats to be controlled by the wall of discrimination because they are intelligent, ambitious, refined, clean, rational, etc. Such opposites can coalesce and evoke hostility in the racist mind only because it is not really any set of behavior traits which constitute the defectiveness of out-races. It is the very being of the out-race which is defective.

The racist is fond of saying to the outsider, "You simply do not understand." He is frequently correct in this judgment. The racist is incorrect, however, concerning that which needs to be understood. He believes that it is the out-race that must be understood in its strange, human deviation. In fact, it is the racist himself who needs understanding. What requires understanding is the idolatrous nature of the commitment which he has made and the pathological nature of his fears and insecurities.

The social, political, and economic effects of the stereotypical system have been observed by many analysts. But only a few have perceived the spiritual effects of stereotyping. An excellent summary of the latter is presented by Kyle Haselden. First, "stereotyping is the symbolic denial of the right to be. If we say that all Negroes are as bad as any Negro and that no Negro is ever any better than all Negroes we have in effect said that there is no such thing as *a* Negro." [31] The stereotype thus denies individuality to the members of the race described. It is the affirmation of the existence of one large, undifferentiated, human mass. This is identical with denial of the human existence of members of out-races, for to be truly human is to be a responsible individual. Stereotypes assert that the hated out-group possesses only a collective, homogenized existence. Since, as Haselden puts it, the mere act of citing some exceptionally able and successful Negro to the rabid racist evokes the reply, "He's still a nigger," it is clear that out-race individuals are inconsequential in the racist consciousness.

The second effect of the use of the stereotype at the spiritual level rests upon the stereotyper himself. The stereotype is "the screen behind which the white man hides in bad conscience or in fearful pride the real Negro." [32] That is, it enables him to blot the Negro out of existence. Consequently he is never obliged to face the real Negro, but can always manipulate the image which he himself has created. In so

[31] Kyle Haselden, *The Racial Problem in Christian Perspective* (New York, 1959), p. 143. [32] *Ibid.*, p. 147.

doing he removes his own sense of justice from his conscience, for the Negro is not permitted the status of fellow man with a claim on his white neighbors. The "I" never encounters the "Thou" because the "Thou" has been made invisible. Only a homogenized mass is present to the "I." The "I" only experiences, appropriates, and manipulates pieces of the homogenized mass which the "I" has created.

In the United States a Negro is forced to be a Negro before anything else and sometimes to the exclusion of anything else. He rarely experiences being thought of or referred to as an American. The appellation "American" may sound strange and new when he hears it applied to himself for the first time in a foreign country. Within his own country, he is a hyphenated American, a Negro-American, a semi-alien. The black nationalism of the Black Muslims is in part a reaction to this condition. The Black Muslim mythology attempts to glorify that from which the Negro cannot escape. The Black Muslims repudiate the white man's manipulated image of the Negro, and proceed to substitute an idealized self-image. Black nationalism thus seeks to find the man whom white racism has destroyed. But it seeks to find him by substituting a manipulated image for a manipulated image. Like white racism, black nationalism also blots the Negro out of existence by losing him in a homogenized mass. Thus counter-racism ends in spiritual defeat. Neither the self nor the other is found.

C. False security in prejudice and uncertainties concerning the image

Prejudice is the mental state which distinguishes the racist consciousness. "Prejudice is a rigid, emotional attitude toward a human group."[33] Obviously, people may have favorable or unfavorable attitudes toward objects with strong emotional quality. But these attitudes are readily modified by new experiences and the presentation of new facts. Prejudiced attitudes, on the contrary, are relatively unmodifiable. The prejudiced person selects cues from new experiences that best fit into old categories and harmonize with stereotypes already formed.

Prejudice involves prejudgment and misjudgment of a human collectivity. People are often anxious to correct misjudgments, but "prej-

[33] George Eaton Simpson and J. Milton Yinger, *Racial and Cultural Minorities* (rev. ed.; New York, 1958), p. 15.

udice is a misjudgment that one defends."[34] An ethnic or racial prejudice is an overcategorization of a whole group of people. It pays little or no attention to individual differences. When individual differences are taken into account and given due consideration, the prejudgments and misjudgments of prejudice are no longer present. This is precisely the thing which the racially prejudiced person cannot bring himself to do. He holds hostile attitudes toward a given person solely because that person is a member of the group toward which he is hostile. Prejudice is "an avertive or hostile attitude toward a person who belongs to a group, simply because he belongs to that group, and is therefore presumed to have the objectionable qualities ascribed to that group."[35]

Whether action is directed toward one member of a group or a multitude of them, the prejudice which prompts action "entails an unwarranted idea concerning [the] group as a whole."[36] The phrase "presumed to have the objectionable qualities ascribed to the group" means that evidence to the contrary is ineffectual. Unless it is the mild conformist type, racial prejudice constitutes judgments that are not reversible by mere exposure to new knowledge. As already stated, prejudice involves misjudgments that one defends. Indeed, the prejudiced person becomes extremely emotional and hostile when his prejudgments and misjudgments are threatened by contradictory pronouncement and evidence. The struggle to preserve the image to which he is already attached is intensified. This must be done, of course, by resorting again to the racist frame of reference. The orientation of his consciousness drives him in one direction—back to the evidence which has already been interpreted in a racist world of discourse. When pushed to what it regards as the limit, the racist consciousness brings discussion to an end with the final affirmation, "Well, after all, a nigger is a nigger" (or, "a white man is a white man").

The security built by prejudice is false; the image created by the racist consciousness is uncertain. The source of the insecurity and uncertainty of the racist consciousness is its understanding of itself. Racist man is never sure of himself. He is continuously afraid. His ideology is in large measure a "whistling in the dark." The self-image of the racist consciousness involves the false security of a man—Gentile or white—

> who imagines himself the ultimate man and judges those who do not conform to his standard of beauty, culture, physiognomy, dil-

[34] *Ibid.* [35] Allport, *op. cit.*, p. 8. [36] *Ibid.*, p. 9.

> igence, laziness, or any other characteristic which he ascribes to himself, for falling short of the ultimate of which he is the exemplar. But there is a certain insecurity here also. This ultimate man has a darkly conscious sense of the fact that he is not as ultimate as he pretends, and that the groups which he pretends to hold in contempt might actually beat him at his own game if he relaxed the restraints which he has placed upon them.[37]

Illustrations of this contradiction in the racist consciousness are numerous. The claim that the Negro is uneducable and incapable of sharing equally in civilization is made by the same people who fear the education of the Negro lest he compete equally or even dominate. The conviction that the Negro cannot make a good soldier, held during the last war, was combined with the fear of his presence once he had returned home. The many claims concerning Negro inability to perform specific functions, particularly in the technological world, are made in conjunction with concerted efforts to deny him opportunity for training and expression in these fields. The feeling of racial superiority is always manifest as a curious compound of insecurity and false security.

It is this contradiction in the racist consciousness which makes a plan of political action an inherent aspect of the racist faith. No matter how powerful the dominant race is in relation to subordinate races, it is never willing to trust its superiority to nature, where it claims its superiority lies. Racist man can never rest at ease. He is really not sure of himself. The claim to an intrinsic superiority of being does not remove a sense of feeling threatened. According to Theodore Newcomb, the one common factor which emerges from all intense character-conditioned prejudice is "threat orientation."

> Attitudes of prejudice correspond to predispositions to perceive the objects of the prejudice in terms of threat, together with predispositions to treat them in ways designed to ward off the threat. People who have strong group prejudices are often not at all clear as to the nature of the threats with which they feel themselves confronted. Nevertheless, their behavior—such as keeping the "outsiders" at a distance, or attempting to injure them—are of precisely the kind that we should expect when situations are perceived in terms of threat. The process of learning to be prejudiced is a part of a process of learning to perceive members of certain groups as sources of threat.[38]

[37] Reinhold Niebuhr, "Christian Faith and the Race Problem," in D. B. Robertson, ed., *Love and Justice* (Philadelphia, 1957), p. 127.

[38] Theodore M. Newcomb, *Social Psychology* (New York, 1950), p. 579.

Members of out-races are not threats in the sense that a criminal who is a would-be killer is a threat. Obviously, a would-be killer is a threat to anyone who has the misfortune of being in his path, and the racial identity of the criminal makes no difference in the objective situation. The paradox in the racist consciousness is its sense of threat in out-races when their behavior and functions are creative and constructive. An ignorant Negro menial, even with a criminal record, confined to the Negro community, is not a serious threat. It is the Negro whose life is characterized by upward mobility who poses a serious threat. Only the Negro of character, self-respect, and achievement is "uppity and dangerous." He has got "out of his place." The Jew is a constant threat not because he is stupid, of low intelligence, and a drag on society, but because he is too intelligent and creative. Negroes in small Southern communities have often found it desirable to minimize their achievements, especially economic achievement, as an accommodation measure. For their very achievements would be taken as evidence that they are threats to the peace and tranquillity of the community.

The consistent tendency to view the contrast conception in terms that are as low as possible is the chief testimony that the racist holds a low estimate of himself. No racist pronouncements have ever glorified out-races. This is precisely the line that such pronouncements ought to take if the greatness of the "superior" race is to be genuinely accredited. Man is in fact so frail and dependent a creature that he is jarred by his own claims to ultimacy. Accordingly, when ultimate man (racist man) attempts to say concretely what he means by his ultimacy, he does not compare himself with superior men or mythological gods. Rather, he contrasts himself with corruption. He constructs a picture of out-races in terms as low and degraded as he can imagine, and proceeds to announce that it is these people to whom he is superior. This is why the racist consciousness must first "know" the other before it can know itself. The racist views himself as the contrast of that which he makes of the other. But his greatness is exceedingly limited because he always "creates" human scum as the opposite pole in the order of human being.

The false security in prejudice and the uncertainty concerning the accuracy of the constructed image are also evident in the racist's preference for escape methods over facing the facts pertaining to the contrast conception. Ignorance of the facts concerning out-races is a valuable escape apparatus. In the United States, the racist combines ignorance of the Negro with the conviction and vigorous affirmation that "we know the Negro." The greater the degree of social distance from the Negro, the clearer the picture of him, and the stronger the conviction that it is correct. In the absence of genuine knowledge, the stereotype is the instrument which fills the gap. Ignorance of the contrast conception thus becomes a negative means to knowledge. Ignorance is a means to knowledge in the sense that it can be relied on never to interfere with stereotyped generalizations by seeking fuller and better information. The Black Muslim approach to the same objective uses opportune ignorance to keep constantly alive the image of the out-race and to reject living dialogue with members of the out-race. Black racists, like white racists, never enter into dialogue with anyone. Racists confine themselves to declarations. They do not ask questions. They do not investigate and analyze. They only provide answers. These answers are always deductions from the racist faith.

Escapism is also found in the claim that no racial problem exists. The diagnosis of the race problem as being no problem suppresses doubt, guilt, concern, anxiety, and disagreement. "A common escape from feelings of guilt is to assert that there is no reason to have them." [39] In race relations this type of escape rationalization takes the form of praise for "our fine, harmonious, and peaceful race relations." Certain stereotypes of the Negro are designed to support this escape rationalization. One often hears such expressions as: Negroes are happier by themselves and in their own churches. Negroes prefer Southern to Northern employers because the Southerners understand them better. Negroes preferred Southern to Northern white officers in the segregated armies of World War II. Actually the South has been obsessed with the race problem for decades. The escape rationalizations which deny that the racial problem exists are a partial expression of that obsession.

When the Negro himself diagnoses race relations as "good," this attitude is also an escape rationalization. It is correlated with the Negro's dependence upon whites for his livelihood, his professional or business success. Such a diagnosis is not a reading from the facts; it is a protective device to escape a peril.

In the North the escape rationalization takes the form of being assuaged by worse conditions in the South. Since World War I, the race problem has increasingly become national in scope. Much has been spoken and written about "who is worse than who" between North and South, while little attention has been given to the eradication of the disease itself.

[39] Allport, *op. cit.*, p. 357.

D. The abortiveness of the racist search for meaning and the self

Racism is an abortive search for meaning and wholeness. It is the one structure of meaning known to man in which man claims his being for himself. Racist man is the prototype of man by himself and for himself.

But the search for the self in terms of the self is doomed to failure. Man cannot find himself by seeking himself. The racist has a vague awareness of this fact, but since his commitment is to himself, he cannot escape from the circle of the self. Despite his pride and commitment to self, he senses that he cannot claim absoluteness and immortality for himself alone. He must therefore seek meaning and absoluteness through the race. Since the race is so much larger and so much more enduring than the self, it may seem to have these qualities. Accordingly, the frustrated Black Muslims in America seek self-identity through affirming their corporate Negroness; and white racists stress their whiteness with fanatical intensity when they are falling on the ladder of success.

A second element, important in the racist search for meaning and the self, is the need to be attached to a power center. Racism is an extreme claim to self-sufficiency, but this is combined with the contradictory tendency to locate the shaping forces of history outside the self, and to see these forces as largely antithetical to the self. Actually, all men are insecure in the world. They are insecure because they are sinners. History as well as nature is uncanny. This uncanniness is due to sin. The racist makes the egregious error of seeking to secure himself in the power of a historical collectivity. Obviously a race lacks centeredness. The racist system of meaning and value must therefore use the power and sanctions of political, economic, cultural, and religious institutions. Since the race views itself as opposed to out-races even to the depth of being, the racist center of power is inevitably hostile and aggressive. It is always antithetical power. Nature has presumably so decreed. If racism is not actually in power, as is the case with the Black Muslims, it cannot fully be itself. It lacks the instruments through which the vital impulse can act. Consequently eschatology must be substituted for political power and action.

The abortiveness of the racist search for meaning and selfhood may be observed by noting the adverse effects this search has upon the self. First, the racist inevitably fails to achieve the fullness of being which he seeks for himself. In a quotation from Herman Bahr, Kyle Haselden writes, "the rich take to opium and hashish. Those who cannot afford them become anti-Semites." Haselden goes on to say, "Thus the bigot relies on his prejudices for intensity of feeling, for an acute awareness of being, for the meaning of life. But prejudice does not give him these things so he returns to his prejudice as an addict." [40]

Not only does fullness of being escape the racist at the level of the inner life, it also escapes him in the human structure of relations in which personality exists.

> There are three conditions of man, three structures of consciousness, and they may be distinguished under the names of "master," "slave," and "free man." Master and slave are correlatives. Neither of them can exist without the other. The free man, however, exists in himself; he has his quality within him, without correlation to anything placed in antithesis to him.[41]

It is through the slave that the master exists for himself, and through the master that the slave exists for himself. In each case, self-consciousness is derived through the other. The one only exists and can only understand himself in relation to the other.

The racist structure of human relationship is an expression of the master-slave correlation. In the structure of relationship which is racist, the other is always an "It"—an object to be experienced, appropriated, and manipulated. The object is objectivized, alienated, and depersonalized in a homogenized mass. But the consciousness which alienates and dominates makes itself a correlate of that which it enslaves.

The second of the adverse effects of the racist search for meaning and selfhood is the failure of the self to find community. The racist community is not genuine community. The central element of community is communion. Communion is manifest in a common task, a shared work to be done. In the racial type of community there is no common work to be done, for there is no object beyond the race in which men can find communion.

[40] Haselden, *The Racial Problem in Christian Perspective*, p. 84.

[41] Nicolas Berdyaev, *Slavery and Freedom*, trans. R. M. French (New York, 1944), p. 60.

> Because it [the racial type of community] is not defined by a work to be done, it will only be able to define itself by its *opposition to other groups*. Therefore it will have essential need of an enemy against whom it will build itself; it is by recognizing and hating its enemies that the political body will find its own common consciousness. And finally, since it must at all costs do something, and tend towards something, this something, which is not a determined object, nor an end in the true sense, will be nothing more than the trend of a movement, or the trend of a dream, an undefined march towards nobody knows what conquests. . . . In the totalitarian-racist conception, the essential and primordial task of the social whole, or rather the trend in which communion inevitably asserts itself, is the political domination of other men.[42]

Insofar as a group defines itself in opposition, as the antithetical correlate of the enemy, the group fails to achieve community. It lacks a common object in which it can both find communion and define its existence meaningfully. It lacks a common end toward which it can drive and give expression to the need of self-transcendency. The racist community is historically committed to negation, for it must draw life from the death or subjugation of "inferior man." Its communion is conducted at the altar of a shared hatred and pride.

Finally, the racist consciousness makes its own clarity of vision an impossibility. The racist consciousness is committed to the perception of an image which serves as an obstruction to vision rather than as a means through which the object is clarified. The contemporary movement of Negro life is not understood by many people of the United States because the image of a pattern of behavior drawn from the plantation economy of the past is imposed on the Negro community. The patterns for the present are the idealized patterns of the past. In urban centers of the United States, the expanding Negro middle class is hidden from view by the persisting image of all Negroes as congenitally uncouth, unwashed, and uninhibited. Racist ideology obscures Negro life and attitudes; it does not describe and explain them. It does this because it must; it is the ideology of devotion, the affirmation of an antithetical faith. Muslim dedication to the idea that all white men are devils, beasts, and oppressors obscures all perception of justice, humanitarianism, and affection expressed in the lives of whites toward nonwhites. All racism—black or white, anti-Semitic and otherwise—regards all members of out-races as racist. Out-races are not only be-

[42] Jacques Maritain, *The Rights of Man and Natural Law*, trans. Doris C. Anson (New York, 1943), p. 40.

lieved to stand poles apart from the in-race in the order of being, the in-race also believes that out-races feel the same antipathy, on the basis of this polarity of being, as the in-race does. Thus out-races are inevitably races "in opposition" as well as "opposite races."

E. The Christian approach to the understanding of the self and the other

The foregoing discussion of the racist understanding of man discloses its naturalistic foundations. Man is understood in terms of that which is below himself—the elements of the world, his animality, specifically his genes. To find out who a man is and the quality of his life, we must inquire into his ancestry. Insofar as the facts are accessible, we must make a careful study of his genealogy. For the question of who a man is, is answered in his genetic structure. Thus the racist understanding of man involves "an inversion of the very order of creation," and runs "directly counter to the divine purpose of grace upon which the whole of creation depends." [43] According to Christian faith, man cannot be understood from below; man must be understood from above. "Therefore," says John Calvin, "we must not commence with the elements of the world but with the Gospel which sets Christ alone before us with His cross and holds us to this one point." [44]

The order of nature is made by God to be subordinate to the life and destiny of man. Man is a part of nature; he is an animal; but his essence is not his animality. The Christian doctrine of creation is a doctrine concerning man's present situation; it is not a mere theory of the past. It tells us that man is not to be understood in terms of a world-continuum. Man is not a cosmic being; his existence is not derived from a natural world order. The presence of man in the cosmos is not a necessity; rather, it is due to an *event*, an event of grace, the creation of God.

When man views and uses his neighbors as essentially children of the world of nature, he throws the order of creation into confusion. Men are thus confused with the elements of the natural world over which God has given man dominion. Further, by extending his rightful dominion over the natural world so that it includes dominion over his neighbor man, man rejects his own destiny and the purposes of grace.

[43] T. F. Torrance, *Calvin's Doctrine of Man* (new ed.; Grand Rapids, Mich., 1957), p. 24. [44] *Ibid.*

The true destiny of man is the worship and adoration of God. But man, the master, seeks to displace God and to glorify himself.

In contrast to all other creatures, man is created in the image of God. He is created through the Word, for the Word, and in the Word of God. The Word made flesh is accordingly the source of our knowledge of the nature of man as the creature of God. In beholding the Word made flesh and only in beholding the incarnate Word do we know that we are born to be the sons of God. Only in Christ does the significance of the image of God in which we are created become clear. Man must know God before he can know himself. He can never understand himself out of himself or from any relation which he bears to the world. His personal existence is not found in any natural characteristics which he possesses. Man is created for responsible obedience to God. His personal being is derived from the call of God and his answering act of obedience. Man can understand himself only when he becomes true man, only when he is renewed in Christ. To know himself as man, man must be known; he must be called into union with true man.

> The nature of the man Jesus alone is the key to the problems of human nature. This man is man. As certainly as God's relation to sinful man is properly and primarily His relation to this man alone, and a relation to the rest of mankind only in Him and through Him, He alone is primarily and properly man. . . . True man, the true nature behind our corrupted nature, is not concealed but revealed in the person of Jesus, and in His nature we recognize our own, and that of everyman.[45]

Man's conformability to God is not by natural means, not by inheritance, not even by an influx of grace substantially understood, but by the spirit through the Word. The image of God is not a natural possession of men. Insofar as the image of God may be referred to as a possession, it is a spiritual possession, above nature and the world. The image is not a natural part of the soul. It is "a reflection by the whole soul of that which the soul is not in itself, and cannot claim to be without contumacy and ingratitude." [46]

It is not possible for man to know himself by seeking to find himself in some intrinsic quality which he possesses. While scientific truth is very useful to us in the understanding of man, the distinctively per-

[45] Karl Barth, *The Doctrine of Creation* ("Church Dogmatics," Vol. III, 2) trans. Harold Knight *et al.* (Edinburgh, 1960), p. 43.

[46] Torrance, *op cit.*, p. 55.

sonal escapes even science. The explanation of man in terms of nature, even according to the most exacting demands of science, is doomed to failure. The animal in man is quite real, but if that is all that is in him, he is not man. Science must employ classificatory generalizations, but the truly personal is unrepeatable and recoils from class generalizations. The search for the self by way of introspection also fails to deliver the self. Knowledge of the self in terms of the self is not possible by any route. It is not sufficient to abandon the naturalism of racist ideology only to substitute for it the analysis of nature as required by authentic science. But it is also not sufficient to follow the route of introspection of the psychical sciences. Man is not the creature by himself and for himself. He is the creature from God and for God and he can only be understood by looking at God.

The racist-collectivist view of man is a snare and a delusion. Like the communist doctrine of man, it is a politicization of truth. It presents man with an official view of man. Both the self and the other must be understood according to prescribed images and in the light of the fundamental tenets of an official orthodoxy. The self and the other are placed and made stationary by the requirements of a system of self-glorification. The dynamics of personal and group life must therefore continuously escape racist perceptions. Racist knowledge of the self and the other is controlled and structured knowledge. The self and the other are never permitted to meet and address each other in a fresh encounter. When they meet, they must assume the posture of "I" and "It," and must speak to each other in a prescribed, doctrinaire language. The racist faith requires that the in-race and out-races live, move, and have their being in relationships that reflect "the order of nature." According to this order, they are opposites. When the racist faith is embodied in a power structure, the political expression of the faith takes the form of the imposition of isolation, deprivation, and subordination upon out-races. The antithetical consciousness of racism is thus embodied in human relations, and truly personal relations are made impossible.

The true knowledge of the other person can come only when personal contact is established. Genuine personal knowledge is the product of communion. We come to know others when we enter into living, personal relations with them. The racist structure of living is the very antithesis of the requirements of both self-knowledge and knowledge of the other. Knowledge of oneself is knowledge of oneself in relation to another. Through the "Thou" a man becomes "I." Only as "I" allow the other to confront me as "Thou" do "I" stand before him as "I." When he becomes "It" to me, "I" become the correlate of "It." "I become through my relation to the Thou; as I become I, I say Thou." [47]

To recognize the other as a person is to become aware that he has a claim upon me. He is my brother man. He is the covenant partner, whom God has given to me. To fail to recognize this God-given claim is to put people in the class of things. Each man becomes an "It," an instance of a type. This is what racism does. Members of out-races have no claims upon members of in-races as persons. The former are "hands"—domestics, porters, cotton pickers, etc. The only point of human connection is functional, not personal. But in this very act the racist puts himself in a class of things—bosses, "captains," foremen, white men, etc. Persons remain unknown and invisible for there is no communion. There is no being grasped from above. Racist man neither knows himself nor the other, for man knows himself only as he is known.

[47] Buber, *I and Thou,* p. 11.

CHAPTER III

Person and Community

A. Nature as the foundation of man's essential being

In the analysis of the racist consciousness, the conclusion was reached that the basic racist affirmation of superiority, on the one hand, and inferiority, on the other, is a proposition concerning man as a child of nature. The racist doctrine of man is an unqualified naturalism. To the casual observer this is not evident because racists constantly appeal to historical and cultural demonstration to "prove" the superiority or inferiority of races. The racist apparently convinces himself that his generalizations are empirical until he is obliged to face one exception after another. Then he answers his interlocutor in "definitive" terms. The response usually goes something like this: "Well, I don't care what you say about Sam's character, scholarship, or achievements, he is still a nigger." Or, if the person in question is a Jew, the punch line is, "He is still a Jew." Thus all the alleged "demonstrations" rest on a prior and deeper conviction of human corruption. Sam is a threat to all "decent people" because of his Negroness or his Jewishness.

The objection may be raised that while the fundamental racist proposition is naturalistic, it is not this form of the proposition that is shared by Christians. It is true that Christian racists do not explicitly state, with naturalistic-racist philosophers, that man owes his existence to nature. Christian racists affirm that all men are the creatures of God. But they say this when they are thinking and speaking abstractly. If the races are under discussion, or if decision and action are called for in race relations, the Christian racist resorts to the language of "blood," "nature," "mongrelization," "racial disaster," etc., in exactly the same manner as any secularist does.

In his monumental study of the Negro in the United States, Gunnar Myrdal found everywhere in white America a vulgarized pre-Darwinian and Darwinian evolutionism applied to race.[1] When environmental factors are taken into account in human development, they are either discounted or applied in a loose way. The prevailing racistic evolutionism assumes that culture is transmitted in the genes and that the Negro race is hundreds or even thousands of years behind the white man in "development." But since the genetic constitution of the Negro is presumed to be inferior, a biological ceiling hovers above his head. It is alleged that the improvement of the mind of the Negro race cannot be made beyond a given level. The backwardness of Africa is offered as historical and cultural "proof" of the Negro's natural potential.

Myrdal also found a mysterious, irrational element in the white man's concept of the Negro that is analogous to primitive ideas and practices of taboo. This element cannot be explained in terms of biological or cultural differences. But since it is evoked by the metaphor "blood" and is verbalized by much atttention to ancestry and physical contact, it would seem to belong to the structure of belief that the essence of man is the genetic structure. Whites whose minds are characterized by this magical influence believe that a person who has the smallest drop of "Negro blood" is smitten by a hideous disease; and they possess an indubitable "sense" and "feeling" that they are superior to every single Negro.

The following six points are presented by Myrdal as "the ordinary white American's ad hoc theory on the Negro race:"

(1) The Negro people belongs to a separate race of mankind.
(2) The Negro race has an entirely different ancestry.
(3) The Negro race is inferior in as many capacities as possible.
(4) The Negro race has a place in the biological hierarchy somewhere between the white man and the anthropoids.
(5) The Negro race is so different both in ancestry and in characteristics that all white peoples in America, in contradistinction to the Negroes, can be considered a homogeneous race.
(6) The individuals in the Negro race are comparatively similar to one another, and, in any case, all of them are definitely more akin to one another than to any white man.[2]

The doctrine that man owes his existence to nature and that nature alone determines his essence is given unequivocal expression by the

[1] Gunnar Myrdal, *An American Dilemma* (New York, 1944).

[2] *Ibid.*, pp. 103–104.

naturalistic-racist philosophers. A major misconception of our time, writes Adolf Hitler, is the idea that man conquers nature.[3] Actually man discovers everything and invents nothing. It is by means of the discovery of nature's secrets and laws that man has become master of those other living beings which lack such knowledge. Man's higher existence is due to the ruthless application of nature's laws. Outstanding among the principles of nature's working is "the inner seclusion of the species of all living beings on earth." That is, "every animal mates only with a representative of the same species. The titmouse seeks the titmouse, the finch the finch, the stork the stork, the common mouse the common mouse, the wolf the wolf, etc." [4] If the principle of the inner seclusion of the species is violated, nature imposes penalties. She denies "the bastards further procreative faculty, or she limits the fertility of the coming offspring; but in most cases she takes away the capacity of resistance against disease or inimical attacks." [5] Nature wills to breed life as a whole toward a higher level. Any crossing of races is a contradiction of nature's will and is certain to bring disaster to the perpetrators of this "sin." "Man, by trying to resist this iron logic of Nature, becomes entangled in a fight against the principles to which alone he, too, owes his existence as a human being. Thus his attack is bound to lead to his doom." [6]

The explanation of human essence in terms of biology and of the germ-plasm is set forth nowhere more explicitly than in the work of Lothrop Stoddard. The basic feature of the life process is as follows:

> The new individual consists from the start of two sorts of plasm. Almost the whole of him is body-plasm—the ever-multiplying cells which differentiate into the organs of the body. But he also contains a germ-plasm. At his very conception a tiny bit of the life stuff from which he springs is set aside, is carefully isolated from the body-plasm and follows a course of development entirely its own. In fact, the germ-plasm is not really a part of the individual; he is merely its *bearer,* destined to pass it on to other bearers of the life chain.[7]

Until about a generation ago, says Stoddard, the life stuff was erroneously thought to be a product of the body. But every fresh biological discovery is now revealing the tremendous power of hered-

[3] Adolf Hitler, *Mein Kampf* (New York, 1940), p. 393.

[4] *Ibid.*, p. 389. [5] *Ibid.*, p. 390. [6] *Ibid.*, pp. 392–393.

[7] Lothrop Stoddard, *The Revolt against Civilization* (New York, 1922), pp. 34–35.

ity in the life process and the marvelous potency of the germ-plasm. While modern biology must be dated from the publication of Darwin's *The Origin of Species by Means of Natural Selection*, published in 1859, it was Francis Galton who founded the science of "eugenics" or "race betterment." Galton "announced clearly that heredity rather than environment was the basic factor in life and the prime lever of human progress." [8]

At every stage of its development, the germ-plasm follows its predetermined course. It is carefully isolated and guarded against all external influences. Noxious influences, like chemical substances and disease toxins, are not prime causes of racial degeneracy, as was once supposed. The injury which these influences may cause to the germ-plasm is only temporary. Likewise, unfavorable prenatal influences do not injure or alter the germ-plasm. And once birth has occurred, and the individual is out in the world, environmental influences affect only his body-plasm. They do not fall upon his germ-plasm.

Stoddard concludes

> that man is moulded more by heredity and less by environment than any other living creature, and that the vast differences observable between human beings are mainly predetermined at the instant of conception, with relatively little regard to what happens afterward.[9]

B. Natural being, the source of character

The idea that man is an embodied spirit is reversed in racist anthropology in favor of the view that man is a body who expresses himself spiritually. What a man becomes culturally and spiritually has its basis exclusively in his genetic structure. The hereditary ground of man's being is the source of all virtue and creativity on the one hand, and all vice and destructiveness, on the other. In the racist faith, the problem of human existence is the lack of "right" birth; it is not the lack of rebirth. It follows that the whole human problem is transcended in some persons, namely those members of the alleged superior race whose ancestral line is uncontaminated.[10]

The cultural creativity of the Aryans and the "parasitism" of Jews,

[8] *Ibid.*, p. 42. [9] *Ibid.*, p. 48.

[10] The problem of human existence is sin and finitude. Finitude is not a problem in itself, but it is a problem for sinful man. It sets limits on self-glorifying man who is satisfied with nothing short of being God.

writes Adolf Hitler, are due to the natural "racial" qualities of these two groups. The Jew is destructive because "life urges the Jew towards the lie, that is, to a perpetual lie, just as it forces the inhabitants of northern countries to wear warm clothes." [11] If Jews deny their inner nature, which is to be a people with definite racial qualities, in the long run they can only succeed in leading their existence as parasites among other peoples, Hitler continues. In order to divert disagreeable attention from his person, the Jew must create the false impression that his is not a people but only a religious community. With this start the Jew propagates the first great lie that he is a German, a Frenchman, an Englishman, or some other national. The fact is the Jews have always been a people with definite racial qualities. They are not and never have been a religious community.

> . . . Resulting from his own original nature the Jew cannot possess a religious institution for the very reason that he lacks all idealism in any form and that he does not recognize any belief in the hereafter. But in the Aryan conception one cannot conceive of a religion which lacks the conviction of the continuation of life after death in some form.[12]

The Jewish faith is odious from Aryan viewpoints. It lacks moral value, and is racistic and economic in objective. The religious doctrine of Judaism is directed primarily toward the preservation of purity of blood among the Jews. The life of the Jew "is really only of this world, and his spirit is as alien to true Christianity, for instance, as his nature was two thousand years ago to the Sublime Founder of the new doctrine." [13]

Upon the foundation of this first and greatest lie that the Jew is not a race but a religious community, additional lies are built. Among these is the lie involved in the Jewish use of language. The Jew uses language to hide thoughts rather than to express them. "When he speaks French, he thinks Jewish, and when he turns out German poetry, he only gives an outlet to the nature of his people." [14] The fact that the entire existence of the Jew is based on a continuous lie "is shown in an incomparable manner and certainty in the 'protocols of the Wise Men of Zion.' " [15]

[11] Hitler, *op. cit.*, p. 420. [12] *Ibid.*, pp. 421–422. [13] *Ibid.*, pp. 422–423.

[14] *Ibid.*, p. 423.

[15] This tract was already known to be a forgery many years before Hitler came to power. It was circulated in Germany during his regime and has circulated from time to time in other countries, including America. It purports to "prove" that "international Jewry" aims to destroy Christianity, overthrow governments, and destroy the world.

In contrast to the Jew, the Aryan is the prototype of man. He is the creator of almost all that is worthwhile in human culture. Upon this fact the conclusion must be based

> that he alone was the founder of the higher humanity as a whole, thus the prototype of what we understand by the word "man." He is the Prometheus of mankind, out of whose bright forehead springs the divine spark of genius at all times, forever rekindling that fire which in the form of knowledge lightened up the night of silent secrets and thus made man climb the path towards the position of master of the other beings on this earth.[16]

In France, anti-Semitism takes the form of Manichaeism. All of the evil in the universe, writes Sartre in his study of anti-Semitism, is localized in the Jew. The Jew is believed to be bad by "nature." "For the anti-Semite, what makes the Jew is the presence in him of 'Jewishness,' a Jewish principle analogous to phlogiston or soporific virtue of opium." [17] Sartre believes that this is a primitive horror feeling based on a metaphysical essence. It is analogous to the primitive feeling of taboo which many white persons in America possess toward Negroes. In the anti-Semitic consciousness, the Jew is the embodiment of evil. Driven by a metaphysical principle, he is free only to do evil under all circumstances, even if it destroys himself.

Since the Jew is evil by nature, but manifests the whole range of human virtue and vice in his actual life, he is obliged to live under a double reputation. When he gains a reputation for honesty, this reputation is added to his primary reputation of being a Jew. The Jew is never merely an *honest person*, but always an *honest Jew*. He cannot be an honest or an avaricious person because he is not merely a person. He is always a person and a Jew.

Even when the Jew is permitted to be a free citizen, as in France, the character of human relations which results when these attitudes are controlling and directing has the nature of spiritual tragedy. Sartre provides a poignant description of the experience of a Jew as a citizen of great distinction:

> He is nobody's slave; he is a free citizen under a regime that allows free competition; he is forbidden no social dignity, no office of the state. He may be decorated with the ribbon of the Legion of

[16] Hitler, *op. cit.*, pp. 397–398.

[17] Jean-Paul Sartre, *Anti-Semite and Jew*, trans. George J. Becker (New York, 1960), p. 37.

> Honor, he may become a great lawyer or a Cabinet minister. But at the very moment when he reaches the summits of legal society, another society—amorphous, diffused, and omnipresent—appears before him as if in brief flashes of lightning and refuses to take him in. How sharply must he feel the vanity of honors and of fortune, when the greatest success will never gain him entrance into that society which considers itself the "real" one. As a cabinet minister, he will be a Jewish cabinet minister, at once an "Excellency" and an untouchable. And yet he never encounters any particular resistance; people seem, rather, to be in flight before him; an impalpable chasm widens out, and, above all, an invisible chemistry devaluates all that he touches.[18]

The democrat, writes Sartre, comes to the defense of the Jew. But in so doing, the democrat saves the Jew as abstract, universal man, and annihilates him as Jew. Like the anti-Semite, he fails to encounter the Jew as concrete person. "In contrast to the anti-Semite, the democrat is not afraid of himself; what he fears is the great collective forms in which he is in danger of being disintegrated." [19] Taking this point of view, he fears all forms of the collective consciousness, including the awakening of the "Jewish consciousness." To prevent such an awakening, the democrat must insist that individuals really exist in an isolated state, and "there is no Jewish question." Thus the democrat destroys Jewishness. In order that the Jew may exist as a man, he must cease to exist as a Jew. But when he does, he lacks the concrete particularity which is human existence. The anti-Semite wishes to destroy the Jew as a man and to leave him as a Jew, an untouchable, an object of his own creation. The democrat wishes to destroy the Jew as a Jew, thus leaving him an "abstract and universal subject of the rights of man and the rights of the citizen." [20] In both cases the concrete person is annihilated.

There is a striking analogy between the experience of the Jew in France and that of the Negro in America in relation to the two types of consciousness just described. Frequently those who consider themselves to be defenders of the Negro against clear and overt expressions of hostility admit that they must first translate Negroes into white men before they can accept them as persons, even at the level of consciousness.

Sometimes a Negro is given a guided tour along the path of consciousness, leading to the point of his recognition as a full-fledged

[18] *Ibid.*, pp. 79–80. [19] *Ibid.*, p. 56. [20] *Ibid.*, p. 47.

human being. He is taken aside by a white person, often at a Christian conference, and given a step-by-step account of "how I overcame prejudice" or "how I resolved the issue for myself." The narrator begins by admitting in effect and unwittingly that the Negro is a contrast conception to him and that there seems to be a fundamental wrongness in the Negro's being. He then may continue as follows: "After many years of sharing prevailing attitudes toward the Negro, I met a fine, charming, and cultivated Negro person. Prior to this experience I had only known Negroes as servants and menials and had thought that these were their natural roles. After this initial experience, graduate school and professional contacts have made it possible for me to meet more educated Negroes. At first, I reacted in the traditional way, by simply explaining cultivated Negroes as 'different.' But gradually, helped by reading, lectures, and associations, I came to realize that individuals differ within all groups. Now, I find it easy to accept a Negro as an individual. I simply say to myself, 'He is just like me, after all. He is cultivated, refined, and charming in spite of being a Negro.' In short, I forget about his being a Negro, and think of him culturally as being like me." The narrator of such accounts, even though Christian, never realizes that he has annihilated the being whom God created and translated that being into his own image. He has done this because, even though he regards himself as "advanced" in his racial thinking, he is still committed to the faith that authentic humanity can inhere only in Caucasianness. It cannot inhere in Negroness. To be genuinely man is to be Caucasian. When therefore a non-Caucasian manifests attributes expected of the finest men, he must be thought of as Caucasian. A special image must be created for him.

Unashamed anti-Negroism, of course, explicitly proclaims that Negroness cannot be the foundation of fine character. The heart of the Southern credo, says Howard Odum, is that "the Negro is a Negro and nothing more." [21] This means that he is not the same sort of human being as the white man. In short, he is not human.

Odum presents certain exhibits as evidence of the centrality of the theme in Southern culture that the Negro is not human. The first exhibit is

> the almost universal refrain that "the Negro thinks he can act like white folks; well, he can't do it down here." "These niggers coming back South try to do like white folks. But it don't take us long to

[21] Howard W. Odum, *Race and Rumors of Race* (Chapel Hill, N.C., 1943), p. 22.

put them in their place." "A smart nigger knows better than to try to act like white folks." [22]

A correlative exhibit is found in attitudes toward Negro college graduates. Instead of being proud of them and looking toward their making a contribution to the well-being of the South richer and fuller than their parents could make, Southern whites reserve a special disdain for them. They are regarded as "uppity and trying to do like white folks." [23] A common refrain heard among religious youth in appealing for better treatment for the Negro is: "I know the Negro is just a Negro and must be kept in his place, but he is just as dear in the sight of God as a white person." [24] In practice this means that the ideal of Christian brotherhood simply does not apply to the Negro. The Negro is loved by God and is equally worthful in God's sight as the white man, and this important religious idea ought to be borne in mind—but in practice, the Negro must be kept in his place. The fatherhood of God and the brotherhood of man are basic planks in the total religious platform—"but the Negro, that is different. You don't understand. He is the Negro. No, we can't worship with him, work with him, vote with him, associate with him. Don't you understand? It just isn't done. It just can't be done." [25]

All these exhibits indicate the strength of the belief that there is something permanent and enduring in the Negro's being which is negative in character. This negative factor denies him the possibility of authentic human expression, and makes him unworthy of sharing in genuinely human community. Where the concrete reality of this negative factor is sought after, it is declared to be "blood" and the genes.

The counter-racism of the Black Muslims is based on a perversion of Islam. Unlike the Christian whites, the Black Muslims are able to elaborate an explicit racist doctrine of man directly from their fundamental religious claims. But as in the case of all racism, the Black Muslims are obliged in the end to distinguish between the races on naturalistic grounds. The dichotomy which they see in the human race is empirically expressed in color.

In the Black Muslim mythology, Allah is the principal being of the divine reality, but Allah is not a Godhead complete in himself.

> All Black men represent Allah, or at least participate in him, for all black men are divine. . . . pure Black is equivalent to Absolute perfection. . . . All colors are but shades of black; white is

[22] *Ibid.* [23] *Ibid.*, p. 25. [24] *Ibid.*, p. 23. [25] *Ibid.*

but the absence of color; hence the white man is incomplete and imperfect. All things that are, are made by man; and only Black Man is truly wise and creative.[26]

C. The racist denies himself and his victim wholeness of person

Racism creates two or more homogeneous, dichotomous groups of human beings. When the racist consciousness is at work, the "we" constitutes one collective being without distinction as to qualities, characteristics, values, and purposes; and the "they" constitutes one collective being without distinction as to qualities, characteristics, values, and purposes, standing in homogeneous contrast to the "we." The "they," of course, may be several groups; but, in the confrontation with the in-race, each out-race is a contrasting collective homogeny.

The racist consciousness strains to find visible characteristics by which it may discern the out-race and sharply distinguish it from the in-race. Visible characteristics are important because they "have a power to over-shadow all other characteristics and to create an illusion of a greater similarity between the individuals of the out-race and a greater difference from the in-race than is actually warranted." [27] This straining after a distinguishing physical mark is expressed in the erroneous notion of "the Jewish nose" and the false claim that "I can always tell a Jew." It reaches its climax in the manufacture of artificial marks for the purpose of making an out-race discernible, as was the policy of the Hitler regime in Germany.

The physical mark is used as an instrument in making the only distinction that is really important—the racial distinction. To the racist consciousness, men are always "black men," "white men," "Aryans," and "Jews." All men exist as parts of collective wholes and their identities inhere in these collective wholes. A person is not a whole within a community; he is a part of a homogenized mass. The whole person, possessing self-identity, is unknown to the racist consciousness because the ground of being is not God, the universal ground, but the race—a form of particularity.

In democratic, individualistic American culture, racists constantly appeal to individualism to justify their racist-collectivist practices. They oppose every proposal directed toward the removal of racial re-

[26] C. Eric Lincoln, *The Black Muslims in America* (Boston, 1961), p. 73.

[27] Myrdal, *op. cit.*, p. 98.

strictions in public institutions, public accommodations, and public policy by representing these as areas in which private decisions are being made. As a counterproposal, the racists recommend the continuation of the nonfreedom of out-races in the name of the freedom of individual members of the in-race, expressed as freedom of association, the right to choose one's customers, the right to express one's preferences, etc. The fact is, the racist is supporting the final form—among all the systems—of compulsive collectivism. Racism has no affinity whatsoever with individualism; it is a system of compulsion which, when challenged, quickly rises to fanatical proportions. It is the final form among other systems of compulsion—such as communism and extreme nationalism—because it compels in-membership and out-membership on the basis of ancestry. Every white man must conform to the prescribed mores simply because he was born white, whether such conformity harmonizes with his religious and moral commitment or not. He has no personal choice in the matter in the eyes of the racist. If he does not conform, he will be punished. Similarly, every Negro must accept lower-caste status because he was born a Negro. He has no personal choice in the matter. If he does not conform, he will be punished in a manner appropriate to his lower-caste status. Thus both the racist person and the victim of the racist consciousness are forced to engage in the forms of behavior which express their existence as parts of collectivist wholes.

That which Jews as Jews have in common, writes Sartre, is "the situation of the Jew." They must live in a community "which takes them for Jews." [28] "To know what the contemporary Jew is, we must ask the Christian conscience. And we must ask, not 'What is a Jew?' but 'What have you made of the Jews?' " [29] The Jew has been made a part of a whole, an instance of a type. He is not permitted the status of individuality. The distinctness which he possesses as a person is only quantitative. A Jew is a Jew, and one is the same as another. Likewise, there is no such thing as a Jewish community in the anti-Semitic consciousness. There is no Jewish community because there are no authentic individuals to enter into fellowship.

Not only is the victim of the racist consciousness made a part of a whole and denied individuality, the racist person also makes himself a part of a whole and denies his own individuality. In the context of race relations, the racist can only think of himself and make decisions as a white man, an Aryan, or a black man. His own life has meaning to him only as a part of the racial context. The "masses" are the inevitable

[28] Sartre, *op. cit.*, p. 67. [29] *Ibid.*, p. 69.

product of racism and the racist makes a mass man of himself just as surely as he does his victim. Nicolas Berdyaev is correct in rejecting the view which identifies the "masses" with the working class or with the people. The masses may originate in any of the various classes. The system of social stratification does not define the masses.

> The masses are to be defined not so much by social as by psychological traits. Over against the masses is to be set not some particular class, but personality. A lack of expressed personality, an absence of personal originality, a disposition to swim with the current of the quantitative force of any given moment, an extraordinary susceptibility to mental contagion, imitativeness, repeatability; these must be regarded as the principal traits which distinguish one who belongs to the masses. A man with such characteristics is a man of the masses to whatever class he may belong.[30]

Racism produces the irruption of the masses—vast numbers of people who, instead of expressing personality and freedom, respond excitedly to myths, symbols, shibboleths, and the rantings of demagogues.

As we have already seen, racist self-awareness is a form of the master-slave correlation. That is, consciousness of the self is derived through the consciousness of the other. The racist lacks the awareness of the free man, who is conscious of each individual for himself, and freely goes out from himself to the other. The racist consciousness is antithetical consciousness. It is obliged to alienate, to eject human nature into an external structure, a category. The racist cannot interiorize because his self-awareness is derived from the external object. Thus the racist can never find the center of his own being. Just as those from whom he derives his self-awareness exist for him only as parts of a whole, he exists for himself only as a part of the correlative and antithetical whole. He too must lack individuality. In the context of race relations, the racist lives solely in the "I-It" world. In this world he can never find himself as person, for to live in the "I-It" world alone is not to be real man.

Likewise, the racist collective is not a true community because "only men who are capable of truly saying Thou to one another can truly say We with one another." [31] Genuine community is constituted of free, responsive, and responsible persons. The members of a racist

[30] Nicolas Berdyaev, *Slavery and Freedom,* trans. R. M. French (New York, 1944), p. 121.

[31] Martin Buber, *Between Man and Man,* trans. Ronald Gregor Smith (Boston, 1955), p. 176.

collective exist alongside one another, after the manner of soldiers under command. The content of the command consists in those values by which the group esteems itself and those sanctions by which it preserves itself. The members of the collectivity are "creative" only insofar as they are obedient and conformist. They are valuable only as parts of an organism, not as free, responsible persons in community.

D. The Christian doctrine of essential being

The fact that man is a part of the animal kingdom may be thought of as the one thing concerning which he would never boast directly or indirectly. But this is precisely what racism does inadvertently. Insofar as racism is conscious of the Christian doctrine of creation, it must take only one element of that doctrine as important—the fact that man has been created out of the dust of the earth. It is in this element that the kinship of man to the world of nature and animality is attested. But man's creation out of the dust of the earth

> was especially designed to remind him of his creaturehood, and creaturely kinship with the rest of the world, as a curb to his pride and self-exaltation, and lest he should read more than he ought into the fact that he has been made in the image of God.[32]

The Christian doctrine of creation means that man does not have his own existence. Man is not a being of himself and for himself; he is a dependent being. He owes his existence to God, and is held in being at every moment by God. The idea of creaturehood under God must not even be confused with any kind of spiritual substantialism, to say nothing of naturalism. The Christian doctrine of creation is not an affirmation of any kind of intrinsicalness. It is not a theory of the immanence of divinity in man.

> Rather, it means, first of all, that we are creatures, that we are dust and ashes, and that in ourselves we are nothing. It means that in ourselves we have no permanence and nothing whereupon we could base our own right and our own claims, nothing that we ourselves can assert as the meaning and worth of our life.[33]

[32] T. F. Torrance, *Calvin's Doctrine of Man* (new ed., Grand Rapids, Mich., 1957), p. 26.

[33] Rudolf Bultmann, *Existence and Faith*, trans. and ed. Schubert M. Ogden (Cleveland, 1960), p. 176.

When man forgets this, when he fails to give thanks to God and to give Him the glory, he is in fact, nothing. But racism goes beyond forgetting. It is more than the religious indifference, widespread among men. It is idolatry. It is a decisive act of turning away from God to the creature. It is the worship of the creature instead of the Creator (cf. Romans 1:25).[34] Racism is complete self-deification. Other forms of self-deification make absolute some center of power, meaning, and loyalty beyond the individual, with which the individual can identify. Such centers are nations, classes, and cultures. The absolutization of these structures and centers of meaning and loyalty is always connected with the idea of function or historic mission. In short, these centers of meaning and structures of power have "proved" and must continue to "prove themselves." But racist self-deification is devoid of any qualification. It is not a claim based on function and mission; rather, function and mission are referred back to the claim. The being which God has given to man as being in relation to God and man, racist man claims as independent being, as being-for-himself. The racist presumes to procure life by his own power, to live from the self rather than God. Racism is life "according to the flesh." It presumes that man has his life at his own disposal, and also the lives of other men if they are members of out-races. Other men are "my niggers."

What makes man, the creature of God, truly human? We derive our human nature as such from Christ, as well as our actual and potential relationship to God. "For it is He who as the ground and goal of the covenant of grace planned for man, is also the ground and goal of man's creation." [35] Man is made in the image of God. God's gift of the image is an act of pure grace. Man is intended to image the glory of God through responsive obedience and grateful acknowledgment of God's mercy and providence. Thus man's dignity is a received dignity. It is the gift of the image. "Man's dignity is not found by looking at him, but by looking at his creator." [36] The dignity of man is conferred; his worth is bestowed.

> When man enters into the love of God revealed in Christ he becomes truly human. True human existence is existence in the love of God. . . . True humanity is not genius but love, that love

[34] All scriptural references used hereafter are taken from the Revised Standard Version of the Bible (New York, Thomas Nelson & Sons, 1952).

[35] Karl Barth, *Church Dogmatics*, Vol. III, 2, trans. Harold Knight (Edinburgh, 1960), p. 50.

[36] Kyle Haselden, *The Racial Problem in Christian Perspective* (New York, 1959), p. 170.

which man does not possess from or in himself but which he receives from God, who is love. True humanity does not spring from the full development of human potentialities, but it arises through the reception, the perception, and the acceptance of the love of God, and it develops and is preserved by "abiding" in communion with the God who reveals Himself as Love.[37]

While man is a part of the animal kingdom, while he is made of the dust and is accordingly body as well as mind and spirit, nevertheless the distinctively human factor cannot be derived from the biological factor.

> The humanum is, in itself, something which cannot possibly be derived from the animal kingdom. . . . We do not know . . . what kind of brain is required to achieve the simplest human act. . . . The human act is that which cannot be explained from vitalistic motives alone; a human act desires to achieve something mental for its own sake, something beautiful for the sake of its beauty, something good for the sake of goodness, something true on account of its truth, something holy for the sake of holiness.[38]

Christian faith knows that in his aspect as a bodily being, there is no essential distinction of quality between man and other members of the animal kingdom. The peculiar dignity of man and his peculiar creaturehood are derived from the special way in which God relates to man. Man alone among the creatures of the earth was created for fellowship with God and called by Him to responsible obedience.

Not only does the racist doctrine that the biological element is the essential factor in man's being stand in contradiction to the Judeo-Christian doctrine of human essence, but racism stands in opposition to the Judeo-Christian tradition in the understanding of human variation. In the racist understanding of man, racial variation is a fundamental, structural, human differentiation of polar proportions. To differ in race is to differ in essence. On the contrary, the biblical faith affirms the unity of the human race in creation and destiny. Further, the Bible speaks of only one structural differentiation, and that one is within the human race, namely, male and female.

> The so-called races of mankind are only variations of one and the same structure, allowing at any time the practical intermingling

[37] Emil Brunner, *The Christian Doctrine of Creation and Redemption*, "Dogmatics," Vol. II, trans. Olive Wyon (Philadelphia, 1952), pp. 58–59.

[38] *Ibid.*, pp. 80–81.

> of one with the other and consisting only in fleeting transitions from the one to the other so that they cannot be fixed and differentiated with any precision but only very approximately, and certainly cannot be compared with the distinct species and sub-species of the animal kingdom.[39]

Since racism is pseudo-science as well as pseudo-faith, the verdict of genuine science is relevant in this connection. The quotation above from Karl Barth harmonizes perfectly with contemporary genetics and physical anthropology. The races of man constitute one species, *Homo sapiens*. The differences between the races are relative; they are not absolute. The characters which distinguish races are of the same sort as those which distinguish individuals. Races are distinguished from each other by the relative commonness within them of certain inherited characters. The races shade imperceptibly into each other. Great multitudes of the people of the earth are in-betweens. From a scientific viewpoint, where one race ends and another begins must finally be determined by an arbitrary judgment. Further, the very concept of race is dynamic and not static, as race purists suppose. Races do not stay put; they continue to exist as races as long as the original conditions which brought them into being remain. Principal among the conditions for the continuation of a race without change is geographical isolation.

The fact that man is being-in-relation and the fact that he expresses his essence only insofar as he freely responds to God in obedient love means that each man is a unique individual characterized by wholeness. Since racism affirms that nature is the root of personality, it destroys the wholeness and independence-dependence of man. Man is perceived as a part of a whole, a race, which is itself only a part of a whole. And since this part is defined naturalistically, it belongs to the realm of necessity, rather than the realm of freedom. Racist anthropology knows nothing of finite freedom. The driving forces of racist life are instinctive and vitalistic; they are not spiritual. This accounts for the fact that the racists must constantly refer to "the instinctive feeling of revulsion," "natural antipathy," "the feeling of difference," and the "soul force" of Aryanism. It also accounts for the fact that racist philosophers consistently announce that "life is a struggle, a struggle for preservation."

Racist man cannot find wholeness of being through his faith because the ground of being is itself a created element, namely nature. Existence can never be more than its ground. Person and spirit cannot

[39] Barth, *Church Dogmatics*, Vol. III, 2, p. 286.

emerge from nature. And the functions of nature can never be transmuted into spiritual functions except by the spirit. The spirit is the root of personality. Accordingly, the ground and center of man's being lie beyond himself. They are in God. Insofar as he lives, moves, and has his being in God, man is truly human.

E. The Christian doctrine of person and community

God created man in His own image. This is the biblical way of saying, among other things, that man is not a self-sufficient, self-enclosed substance. The center and meaning of man's life lie beyond himself. The meaning and worth of man's life do not reside in him but "in the One who stands 'over against' him, in Christ, the Primal Image, in the Word of God." [40] Man is created in, for, and by love. His very life is an answer. It is responsible existence. He is so created that he must actively receive God's Word to be human.

The Spirit of God bears witness to man's spirit that he is God's son. Thus man's spirit is the root of his personality. Man is created as person in that he must answer God's claim upon him in responsible obedience. To be a person is to be free and responsible. It is to be a whole rather than a part, independent rather than servile. Man is a person who "possesses absolute dignity because he is in direct relationship with the absolute, in which alone he can find his complete fulfillment." [41]

The original divine Word comes to man as grace not as law, as life not as demand. But the original divine Word has been transformed by sin into law. Consequently, man stands before God as a guilty culprit before a judge. He cannot respond to the Word of God in the freedom of responsibility but must live under restraint. When man answers God in Christ, the divine purpose for life is renewed. Life under the law is replaced by the life of grace.

Man is truly man and truly person only if he responds in obedient love to the divine call. He is so created that he has no true life except in God. He is an "independent-dependent" being who can only be himself in free response to the call of God in every detail of his life. The self-determination which constitutes his freedom, however, is a

[40] Emil Brunner, *Man in Revolt*, trans. Olive Wyon (London, 1939), p. 96.

[41] Jacques Maritain, *The Rights of Man and Natural Law*, trans. Doric C. Anson (New York, 1943), p. 4.

secondary self-determination. It is based on the determining power of the Holy Spirit. Conformability to God is the work of the Holy Spirit. Conformability is not produced or maintained by any power inherent in man. It is neither the product of inheritance nor of cultural development. "The strength of the imago dei and its continued maintenance in the believer lie in the Word of God and not in the soul of man. In a real sense the image of God in man is the *communicated* Word in which God's glory shines forth." [42]

As existence-in-love, man is bound to man in the community of love. He can be man only in the community of love; he cannot be man by himself. The essence of man is the covenantal relation established in creation. God's creative act is a covenantal act. The form of humanity is one with another.

> The humanity of Jesus consists in His being for man. From the fact that this example is binding in humanity generally there follows the broad definition that humanity absolutely, the humanity of each and every man, consists in the determination of man's being as a being with others, or rather with the other man. It is not as he is for himself but with others, not in loneliness but in fellowship, that he is genuinely human, that he achieves true humanity, that he corresponds to his determination to be God's covenant partner, that he is the being for which the man Jesus is, and therefore real man.[43]

As existence-in-love, man cannot be man except in community, yet each individual is a distinct being. The Christian view of man is at once a radical individualism and a radical universalism. God created man in, for, and by love. Man is for man. The covenantal community which is given in creation is as wide as creation. But in the same creative act, God calls the individual into existence. Although the form of humanity is one with another, yet the individuality of every man is also God-given. God calls each by his own name (cf. ISAIAH 43:1). He has made of every man a unique, unrepeatable, and unexchangeable being. Every man possesses self-identity.

The essence of human community is the union of persons in love. There is no genuine community except the community of love. The radical universalism of Christian faith means that love knows no boundaries of geography, nation, race, or class. All men live within the sacred bond of the image of God. Having his existence from and in

[42] Torrance, *op. cit.*, p. 58. [43] Barth, *op. cit.*, p. 243.

God, man reflects the love of God in his soul. As the reflection of the love of God, his love extends to all men as brothers. Thus a radical individualism can exist only in conjunction with a radical universalism.

In contradistinction to DeMaistre and Marx, Berdyaev points out that that man is most concrete or real "who displays the greatest mastery over particularism and the greatest attainment of universality." [44] DeMaistre sees concrete man as an assemblage of national traits, asserting that he knows nothing of man in general; he knows only Frenchmen, Germans, Russians, etc. Marx lifts up social class as the distinctive mark of man, affirming that there is no man in general, but only workmen, peasants, bourgeois, etc. In each case, concrete man is himself by virtue of particular traits which in turn are historical accidents.

> The quantity of particular traits may be a sign of poverty, not of riches; that is to say a sign of abstraction. The man in whom the fact exclusively predominates that he is a Frenchman, an Englishman, a German, or a Russian or the fact that he is a nobleman or a bourgeois, a professor or a civil servant, is not by any means an abundant man, and he is not the concrete man *par excellence*. Concreteness is integrality and, therefore, it is not determined by the quantity of particular traits. The most concrete man is the universal man, who overcomes the exclusiveness, the isolation, the self affirmation of national, social or professional traits.[45]

Man tends to glorify and exalt himself on the strength of his exclusive associations and connections—the nation, the race, the party, the profession. But in so doing, he indulges in an impersonal exaltation. Man is finite; he must be born into a particular family; he must grow up in a particular nation; and he must choose a particular or a few kinds of work. But if his spirit is bound and determined by these, his life as a man is truncated. Men must live in particular communities and structures because material, intellectual, moral, and spiritual life are impossible without them. But unless men are driven beyond these boundaries by the promptings of grace, they will live out their days without an awareness of authentic manhood.

The tragedy of racism is that it blocks both the simple needs and realizations at the natural level of existence and the freedom of the spirit. Racism obstructs the fulfillment of men's need of each other at

[44] Berdyaev, *op. cit.*, p. 113. [45] *Ibid.*

all levels of life. It structures antithetical relations in the pursuit of material, intellectual, moral, and spiritual ends. It insists on the assessment of opportunities, needs, values, and even human worth on the basis of race. When it permeates the structures of power, racism allocates a reduced share and often only a pittance of the values of culture—material and spiritual—to out-races. It stimulates and encourages hatred, fear, and pride through the institutions of society to the end of preserving the racist-divisionist system. In effect it denies that man is created in, for, and by love. It calls for the absolutization of an alleged form of natural coherence. It thus produces partial man and impersonal society.

CHAPTER IV

Equality and Inequality

A. The shifting grounds of equality in the American setting

"THAT all men are created equal" was announced as self-evident by the American Declaration of Independence. The philosophical foundation of this claim was the doctrine of natural rights. In drafting the Declaration of Independence, Thomas Jefferson drew upon the social-contract theory formulated by John Locke. According to this theory, men are born with the right to life, liberty, and property. During the early decades of the new nation, the doctrine of natural equality became more and more a matter of practice, and less and less a matter of discussion.

But slavery and race were to prove to be undermining factors. In the first draft of the Declaration, Jefferson had denounced slavery, but the passage was later eliminated. After the Revolution, antislavery societies increased, reaching a total of 130 by 1827. Most of these societies were located in the South. Those who opposed slavery called its practice an unjust violation of the laws of God and nature. The defenders of slavery at first attacked the doctrine of natural equality indirectly by claiming that slavery was a necessary evil. But as the institution evolved, it passed beyond the stage of a necessary evil to that of a positive good. The defenses of slavery accordingly became direct and unequivocal, and appealed to the counterdoctrine of the natural inequality of men.

The mortal blow to the doctrine of natural equality was struck by John C. Calhoun, an outstanding Southern political leader of the first half of the nineteenth century. Calhoun argued that "nothing can be more unfounded and false than the prevalent opinion that all men are born free and equal." [1] He asserted that Negroes are an inferior race and that slavery is justified because it accords with their natural inequality. The institution of slavery lasted only fifteen years after Calhoun's death, but "it was his peculiar lot while losing his cause to win his case." [2] Little was heard of Locke's doctrine of natural equality after 1865, but the doctrine of racial inequality was destined to permeate all American institutions and public policy.

In 1848 the first Women's Rights Convention was held in Seneca Falls, New York. For almost a decade women had been joining antislavery and abolitionist societies. In these gatherings they had heard discussions of liberty and equality and they experienced a growing sense of urgency that these doctrines be applied to themselves. The initiators of the new Women's Rights movement appealed to two grounds of equality—the natural-rights theory and the doctrine of equality before God. Neither of these arguments availed anything. With the exception of the Quakers, the Churches rudely rebuffed the Women's Rights movement and called the leaders "agitators." Public opposition to the women was led by clergymen. By 1860 the women were obliged to shift the grounds of their argument, dropping both the natural-rights theory and the idea of equality before God. The new ground of argument directed attention toward the promise of the future rather than toward an original state of nature. The values which were constitutive of the promise of the future were self-protection, social effectiveness, and self-development. It was on these grounds that women won the right to vote.

After the Civil War, the idea of equality became more and more a promise of the future. The idea became an ideal which required concrete programs. Instead of equality in general, Americans now began to speak of equality of suffrage, equality before the law, and equality of opportunity. The struggle for equality before the law found constitutional support in the Fourteenth Amendment, ratified in 1868. This amendment forbade a state to deny "any person within its jurisdiction the equal protection of the laws." The most rudimentary right of citizenship which the amendment protects is the right to vote; but when given a broad interpretation, it also bans all of the traditional forms of discrimination based on race, sex, religion, and property. Prior to the closing of the Western frontier, equality of opportunity was taken for

[1] Quoted in Meyer Weinberg and Oscar E. Shabat, eds., *Society and Man* (Englewood Cliffs, N.J., 1956), p. 257. [2] *Ibid.*, pp. 257–258.

granted. But with all of the land, the timber, and the minerals in the hands of private owners, equality of opportunity became the chief expression of the equalitarian impulse. While the Churches had rejected the application of the idea of equality before God to the Women's Rights movement, they continued to use the doctrine as the ground of equality in general.

B. The racist affirmation of inequality

While democratic thought on the subject of equality has been oriented toward promise and program, racist thought has adhered rigidly to the doctrine of original nature.

"Nature knows no equality," says Lothrop Stoddard.[3] The word "equality" is not found in nature's lexicon. The law of inequality is universal and inflexible in nature. The evolution of life is a process of differentiation which increases with the ascending stages of life; the higher the stage the more the process of inequality grows. "With an increasingly uneven hand, [Nature] distributes health, beauty, vigor, intelligence, genius—all the qualities which confer on their possessors superiority over their fellows." [4] As we have already seen in Stoddard's thought, the hereditary determinant and foundation of racial superiority is the germ-plasm. Since all the qualities of mind and spirit are rooted in the hereditary determinant, the superiority of one race over another is a superiority of fundamental being. It is a superiority of immutable human factors; it is not a merely temporary cultural dominance of one people over another.

In their study of Old City and Old County, Mississippi, the authors of *Deep South* found that whites generally interpreted the subordinate position of Negroes as due to immutable differences between the races. To the whites the Negro is "a lower form of organism, biologically more primitive, mentally inferior, and emotionally undeveloped. He is insensitive to pain, incapable of learning, and animal-like in his behavior." [5] In short, Negroes belong to a different order of humanity than whites, if they are human at all. When the Negro is spoken of as childish, this means undeveloped; but unlike children, it is assumed that he can never grow to maturity. His undeveloped nature is a fact of his creation.

[3] Lothrop Stoddard, *The Revolt against Civilization* (New York, 1922), p. 30.

[4] *Ibid.*, p. 31.

[5] Allison Davis, Burleigh B. Gardner, and Mary R. Gardner, *Deep South* (Chicago, 1941), p. 16.

In his *Black Monday*, the outstanding guidebook for contemporary American white supremacy groups, Judge Tom P. Brady describes the Negro as somewhere between a human being and an animal, but dangerously close to the animal:

> You can dress a chimpanzee, housebreak him, and teach him to use a knife and fork, but it will take countless generations of evolutionary development, if ever, before you can convince him that a caterpillar or a cockroach is not a delicacy. Likewise the social, political, economical, and religious preferences of the negro remain close to the caterpillar and the cockroach. This is not stated to ridicule or abuse the negro. There is nothing fundamentally wrong with the caterpillar or the cockroach. It is merely a matter of taste. A cockroach or caterpillar remains proper food for a chimpanzee.[6]

Since racism is a form of naturalism, the principal arguments for racial inequality are based in the biological sciences. But many racists are also Christians. It is to be expected, therefore, that some of them would appeal to sacred sanctions for white supremacy. This would especially be true in a religious culture like that of the South. Of course, sacred sanctions are implicit for Christians when they are not explicit because the order of nature is understood by them to be the order of creation. The explicit ascription of Negro subordination to the will of God is usually presented in a defense of the existing caste arrangements. But spokesmen are not generally content with resting the case for white supremacy on a divine ordinance. They go on to affirm, at least implicitly, that God has made the Negro an inferior human being. Therefore, the caste arrangements are a reflection of the order of creation. A statement of the case in the terms of the divine creative purpose was made to the authors of *Deep South* by a physician, although he hedged on an explicit declaration of ordination:

> The way I look at it is this way: God didn't put the different races here to all mix and mingle so you wouldn't know them apart. He put them here as separate races and He meant for them to stay that way. I don't say He put the Caucasians here to rule the world or anything like that. I don't say He put them here to be the superior race; but since they have superior intellect and intelligence, I don't think God would want them to mingle with inferior races and lose their superiority. You know the Negro race is inferior men-

[6] Quoted in James Graham Cook, *The Segregationists* (New York, 1962), p. 17.

> tally, everyone knows that, and I don't think God meant for a superior race like the Whites to blend with an inferior race and become mediocre. I think God put all the different races here for a purpose, the Negro and the Indian and the Chinese, and all of them, and He didn't mean for them to mix. I think I am right in saying that, and my attitude is Christian-like.
>
> There is just something about the different colored races that is a little bit abhorrent to me, not just the Negroes, either. I mean all the colored races, and I think that is the way with most white people; they all feel the same way. When I was in the University, I went to a meeting at one of those student movement things, and there was a girl there from India. She was very dark-skinned you know, black as a Negro. Well, she got up there and did a native dance, or sang a song, or something, and I guess it was good. But you know after she got through I said to a fellow who was sitting next to me, "You know, there's something abhorrent to me about her just because of her color." And he said he felt the same way. I think most people feel that way about it, and that's why I don't think God meant for the races to mix. He made them that way so they wouldn't want to mix.[7]

The question may be asked whether the in-race–out-race relationship is always characterized by the superiority-inferiority claim. The question is legitimate because all out-races are not subordinated. Some are competitive groups who, while they are not free from discrimination, do engage in most of the professional, occupational, and institutional life of the majority group of the society. As participants in the main stream of culture, the charges of mental inferiority, laziness, lack of ambition, etc., are not brought against them. For example, no one claims that the Jew is mentally inferior to the Gentile, that he is not ambitious, that he is not a hard worker, etc. Probably more often than not, it is assumed that the Jew is mentally superior, that his ambition is more potent than that of the Gentile, and that he is the possessor of a very high capacity for concentration upon tasks. Yet anti-Semites do contend that Jews are inferior. What do they mean? They mean that Jews are defective in their humanity. They are inferior as human beings. A Jew may therefore outstrip a Gentile professionally and culturally, but this very achievement is bad because it is his. The cultural and economic subordination and deprivation of the Negro is taken as "proof" that he is inferior in his humanity: the alleged human defectiveness of the Jew permeates his cultural and economic achieve-

[7] Davis, Gardner, and Gardner, *op. cit.*, pp. 16–17.

ments, giving his actions the character of vices, and of destructive events in society.

The dual nature of the stereotypical system bears out this contention. There are two broad categories of stereotypes. One group of stereotypes purports to describe a subordinate group and aims to guide social, political, and economic action to keep them "in their place." The other group of stereotypes purports to describe a competitive group and aims to guide action to minimize and, in extreme cases, to eliminate the threat of the group. Thus a subordinate group, like the Negro, is declared to be lazy, irresponsible, dull, shiftless, and unable to acquire knowledge and skills above rudimentary levels. A competitive group like the Jews are credited with intelligence, but Jewish intelligence is thought of as craftiness.

Thus it may be seen that the very same characteristics which appear as virtues in an in-race appear as vices in an out-race.

> The very same behavior undergoes a complete change of evaluation in its transition from the in-group Abe Lincoln to the out-group Abe Cohen or Abe Kurokawa. . . . Did Lincoln work far into the night? This testifies that he was industrious, resolute, perseverant, and eager to realize his capacities to the full. Do the out-group Jews or Japanese keep the same hours? This only bears witness to their sweatshop mentality, their ruthless undercutting of American standards, their unfair competitive practices. Is the in-group hero frugal, thrifty, and sparing? Then the out-group villain is stingy, miserly, and penny-pinching. All honor is due the in-group Abe for his having been smart, shrewd, and intelligent, and, by the same token, all contempt is owing the out-group Abes for their being sharp, cunning, crafty, and too clever by far. Did the indomitable Lincoln refuse to remain content with a life of work with his hands? Did he prefer to make use of his brain? Then, all praise for his climb up the shaky ladder of opportunity. But, of course, the eschewing of manual work for brain work among the merchants and lawyers of the out-group deserves nothing but censure for a parasitic way of life. Was Abe Lincoln eager to learn the accumulated wisdom of the ages by unending study? The trouble with the Jew is that he is a greasy grind, with his head always in a book, while decent people are going to a show or a ball game. Was the resolute Lincoln unwilling to limit his standards to those of his provincial community? This is what we should expect from a man of vision. And if the out-groupers criticize the vulnerable areas in our society, then send 'em back where they came from. Did Lincoln, rising high above his origins, never forget the rights

> of the common man and applaud the right of the workers to strike? This testifies only, that like real Americans, this greatest of Americans was deathlessly devoted to the cause of freedom. But, as you examine the recent statistics on strikes, remember that these un-American practices are the result of out-groupers pursuing their evil agitation among otherwise contented workers.[8]

As we have seen, stereotypes are propositions with a purpose. They belong to the stream of culture, serving as active ingredients in shaping experience and coloring observations. Sociologists are generally agreed that they tell us much more about the social group which uses them than about those whom they claim to be describing. Hostility toward out-races is really not the result of what out-races do. Out-races are judged to be vicious even at the moment when they do the things which the in-race honors in itself. This strange attitude is possible because the in-race in reality holds out-races to be natural enemies.

Does the racist ideology of the subordinated counter-racist also include the doctrine of the inferiority of the out-race? It does. The Black Muslims teach that whiteness is the naturalistic expression of imperfection. The present historical dominance of the white man is no evidence of superiority, whatsoever. Rather, what the white man has done to the black man from this position of eminence is "proof" that he is inferior. He is inherently beastly and oppressive. Whiteness represents evil and is doomed by Allah. Its very appearance in the order of human reality was a mistake of cosmic proportions.

C. The Christian doctrine of equality

The Christian doctrine of equality is an affirmation of faith. It is not a perception of sight. It is an affirmation of faith because it relates solely to the action of God, and not to the achievements of men or to any intrinsic quality which men may possess. Men are equal because God has created them in His own image and called them to sonship. The Christian doctrine of equality does not draw at all upon measurements of talent and merit. It is a doctrine concerning the creative gift of God.

There is ample evidence in history that men are unequal in knowledge, skill, power, and cultural achievements in general. Most of life is

[8] Robert K. Merton, *Social Theory and Social Structure* (New York, 1949), pp. 186–187.

organized and proceeds on the assumption of these inequalities. Men of sight, rather than faith, are obviously much more impressed and influenced by historically conditioned and structured inequalities than by any doctrines of equality, philosophical or theological. But the conviction that men are equal in some fundamental sense has not been destroyed in the West, despite the ideological claims to the contrary or widespread practices that belie the idea. The Western democracies have developed a relatively high degree of political equalitarianism at the very moment in history when disproportions of power, wealth, knowledge, and skill are great and numerous as never before. An important influence in this development has been Christian teachings concerning man.

When Christian faith speaks of equality, it refers to the action and purpose of God. God has created all men in His own image and called all men to the same destiny. The decision as to whether or not men are equal cannot be made by looking at men; he who would decide must look at God. God alone is the source of human dignity. All men are equal because God has bestowed upon all the very same dignity. He has created them in His own image and herein lies their dignity. Human dignity is not an achievement, nor is it an intrinsic quality; it is a gift, a bestowal. Christian faith asserts that men are equally human; all are creatures and all are potentially spiritual sons of God. Variations in the talents and skills of culture rest upon this fundamental humanness.

Thus Christian faith affirms the unity of mankind. The idea of the unity of mankind is another way of expressing the essential likeness of man. Modern science supports the claim of biblical faith that mankind is a unity, but it is not upon empirical evidence that the biblical conviction is based. The conviction of faith is independent of all scientific results because creation stands above the historical and empirical planes.

> The religious belief in the unity of the human race through the Creation, in and for the Divine image, is completely independent of all biological, palaeontological, scientific results. The story of Adam in Genesis expresses, in historical form, it is true, a fact which in itself is super-empirical and super-historical; the biological genealogical question has very little to do with belief in the unity of the creation. . . . The unity of the divine creation of man lies upon a quite different plane. Humanity is not necessarily a unity from a zoological point of view; it may indeed be composed of different species of differing origin or it may not. It is, however, be-

> yond all doubt a unity, a *humanitas*, "through" *the humanum*, its one origin and its one destiny in God's creative Word and plan of salvation, spiritually given to man by God himself.[9]

It is upon the foundation of the equal humanness of men that democratic rights are established. The American Declaration of Independence asserts that "all men are created equal." This proposition was never intended to mean that all men are equal in capacity, knowledge, and skill. Yet it does have concrete political significance. It means that there are some rights that belong to persons as persons, as creatures of God. These rights are said to be inalienable for the very reason that they belong to every person as a person. They can no more be transferred from one person to another than personhood itself can be transferred. And to deny these rights is identical with denying the reality of the person. Inalienable rights are primal. They exist prior to the performance of any function, and are the foundation upon which all secondary and derived rights are elaborated. The rights of the individual as man are primary and unique. All particularized rights are secondary and derived. They derive from the social organization of life and belong to persons only in the exercise of their particular technical, professional, and institutional functions.

Not only does the idea of equal human dignity place the stress on the likeness and unity of mankind and thus constitute the foundation for all assessment of human rights; it also combines harmoniously with unlikeness and inequality. The essential rights of the individual are primary and universal; but individual rights combine harmoniously with derived and differentiated rights relating to historic function because individuality and community are equally original in God's creative act. Man is the covenant-partner of God and of man from the creation. But each man is also created a unique being, with his own individuality. Thus equal dignity and likeness are united with individuality and unlikeness in the Christian doctrine of creation.

The Christian doctrine of individuality and unlikeness is radically opposed to racist particularism. In the Christian idea, individuality means unlikeness and inequality in community. But in the racist idea, individuality does not exist: the individual is made faceless in a homogenized collectivity. Unlikeness and inequality are alleged to be characteristics of racial collectivities rather than individuals. While even the racist is obliged to admit the reality of inequality and unlikeness within races, it is only the alleged inequalities between races that

[9] Emil Brunner, *Man in Revolt*, trans. Olive Wyon (London, 1939), p. 333.

have significance for him. Christian faith knows of unlikeness and inequality only as between individuals. But since individuality is always related to community which is also original in God's plan for man, inequality and equality are harmoniously combined.

The Christian conception of equality is inseparable from the idea of person in community. The two elements of equality and inequality, of equal dignity and different function, are both fully expressed. They are brought together in the Christian idea of communion. The fact that men are different from each other means that they are dependent on each other. In a Christian community, men will to serve each other in their mutual dependence. The one recognizes his dependence upon the other, no matter how lowly the occupation of the other may be in the eyes of the world. There are so many respects in which one man may be superior or inferior to another that there is probably no man who is superior or inferior to another in every respect. The unity of mankind is made the more manifest by the inequalities which have their basis in individuality.

The Christian idea of the unity of mankind finds concrete expression in societies of mutual cooperation and helpfulness. Differences of function create of necessity variations in status and role in institutional structures. But the roles and statuses in these institutions are assigned on the strength of real individual differences. They are not, as in racism, based upon hostile power arrangements, upon the results of previous discriminations, or upon invidious comparisons that falsify the nature of man as a creature of God.

D. The Christian approach to equality and inequality in sociocultural life

The meaning of the Christian doctrine of equality for life in the structures and processes of history has already been foreshadowed in the previous discussion. We must now move from definition more specifically to application.

The fundamental rights of man are the rights of the person. Derived and secondary rights are specialized, occasional, and inseparable from function. They belong to a person only as he functions; they exist in addition to the rights which belong to man as a person.

Derived and secondary rights are alienable. For example, a Senator in the United States enjoys immunity from libel and slander suits when in the line of his duties he brings a charge against a citizen. But senatorial immunity inheres in the office rather than the person. A Senator possesses this immunity only in the line of his senatorial duties, and when he ceases to be a Senator he no longer wears the cloak of immunity. Since his successor immediately puts on the cloak, the right to senatorial immunity is alienable. It transfers from person to person with the transfer of office.

The ideal that "all men are created equal" is incorporated in all the laws of America insofar as those laws reflect the Constitution. Thus statutory laws make the judgment that men are equally persons, whether they be thought of individually, or as races, classes or religious groups. The Constitution at this point is in accord with Christian teaching. The equality which the founding fathers of America intended

> does not depend upon achievement tests, educational progress, or upon scientific findings of any kind. The Negro's right to equal treatment before the law rests upon the single and simple fact that he is a man as other men. Men are not created equal in ability but they are equally men, and are to be treated as equals before the law.[10]

The Universal Declaration of Human Rights of the United Nations has perhaps stated as precisely as any document what classes of differences among men admit of differential treatment and what classes of differences do not admit of differential treatment. Obviously, a United Nations publication cannot intend to be a Christian document, but its ethical conclusions may, as in this case, harmonize with Christian motives and perspectives. Differential treatment is admissible and justified when it is based on the following two classes of differences:

> a) differentiations based on conduct imputable to the individual—examples: industriousness-idleness, decency-indecency, merit-demerit; and
> b) differentations based on individual qualities that in spite of not being imputable to the individual have a social value—examples: physical and mental capacities, talent, innate ability, and the like.[11]

Differential treatment is not admissible and justified when it is based on the following two classes of differences:

[10] T. B. Maston, *Segregation and Desegregation* (New York, 1959), p. 51.

[11] Quoted by Alfred Schutz, "Equality and the Meaning Structure of the World," in *Aspects of Human Equality*, Lyman Bryson *et al.*, eds., p. 68.

a) grounds which are not imputable to the individual, and which should not be considered as having any social or legal meaning: such as color, race, or sex; and

b) grounds of social generic categories such as language, political or other opinion, national or social origin, property, birth, or status.[12]

The fact of individual differences of talent and gifts is viewed with the utmost seriousness by Christian faith because the individual is a reality in God's creative act. But Christian teaching stands in radical opposition to all aristocratic tendencies in its stress on the responsibility of those who possess superior gifts and have been the beneficiaries of superior opportunities. Those who have superior gifts and cultural acquisitions have for that very reason correspondingly more responsibility. Superior power, wealth, and knowledge do not mean greater privilege, but greater responsibility. In Christian teaching, equality is an imperative of love, directed to persons without reference to their varying capacities. But since equality is an imperative of love, it is all the more concerned about the weak whose need is greatest. Just as a good parent seeks to equalize any deficiencies which nature may have imposed on one of his children, Christian love equalizes any inequality which nature may have left in the family of man. Christian love is creative and spontaneous. It renders service to those who are weak in humble self-giving. It knows nothing of paternalistic pride and demands no glory.

The tendency to combine superior power, knowledge, technology, and skill with systems of domination, exploitation, cruelty, and pride has been a perennial sin of fallen man. Racism has been the outstanding expression of this tendency in the modern world. When collective man transmutes his gifts and opportunities into power, he perennially uses this power as the basis of self-exaltation and domination, rather than service and the uplift of others. Superior technologies and the opportunities that are derived therefrom have historically meant imperialistic power and privilege, not responsibility and service. But man has seldom admitted that his might has made right. The more man glorifies himself, the more blatant are his claims to virtue. At the very moment when imperialism and slavery were at their height, modern nations made their loftiest pronouncements concerning the civilizing process, evangelism, and service. "Dread and terrible are they; their justice and dignity proceed from themselves" (HABAKKUK 1:7).

[12] *Ibid.*

Even if the claims to superiority of racist man and those of all ruling classes were true, the political claims drawn from these claims remain grossly immoral. Jacques Maritain speaks eloquently on this matter:

> If, finally, there are in the rule of providence over man unequal historical vocations for nations and for great ethnic groups, if there are divine preferences, if the blessing of the forefathers have poured on human progeny unequal abundance, all these are inequalities in *fact* and not by *right* and depend at bottom on divine freedom. They do not break the unity of the human family, but attest in it that diversity which goes with the proper condition of the created and which demands to be perfected in mutual aid and compassion; and they are written into history naturally and spontaneously by the very operation and use of the allotted gifts. To see in them the expression of essential necessities and constitutive laws which the knowledge and power of man are to exploit in order to assure his domination over the universe, is a chimera and presumptuous pride.[13]

The Christian faith has been the informing power of what Karl Barth has called the intentions and desires of democracy.[14] The idea of equality in democracy has maintained a purity of content insofar as its various functional expressions have rested on the idea of equality of person. The doctrine of the equality of persons belongs to the Judeo-Christian tradition. Men are equal in their essential and common humanity. Any concrete decision concerning public policy, any proposed legislation, or any judicial decision relating to a question of equality must take as its starting point the equality of persons. The fact that the idea of equality before God has not had a great political potency must be charged against the Churches. We have already observed that the concept of equality before God along with the doctrine of natural right, had to be abandoned by the Women's Rights movement of the last century because these doctrines proved ineffectual. Repeatedly, Churchmen have emptied the doctrine of equality before God of all sociohistorical content. They have confined its meaning almost exclusively to the plan of salvation, with an occasional reference to "creation in the image of God." By placing all of the meaning of equality before God in the context of the plan of salvation, the judgment con-

[13] Evans and Ward, eds., *The Social and Political Philosophy of Jacques Maritain* (New York, 1956), p. 62.

[14] *Against the Stream: Shorter Post-War Writings, 1946–1952* (New York, 1954), p. 44.

cerning the equality of men is abstracted from history and deposited solely in the mind of God. Obviously this is a falsification of the meaning of the life of faith and man's covenant relationship to God. The man of faith is grasped; he is possessed; God reigns in him; the mind of Christ is in him. His life is thus converted and turned around; it proceeds from God. His judgments are henceforth according to the mind of Christ. That which is equal before God cannot but be equal to him.

Furthermore, it must be observed that if equality is not a historical relationship, it has no meaning at all. In the kingdom of God men do not exercise lordship the one over the other. In the kingdom, men do not even marry and give in marriage. The whole question of preferences, hierarchies, and inequalities is irrelevant to the kingdom of God. A Christian discussion of equality and inequality has to do with man before God in history, or it is a meaningless discussion.

The doctrine of equality before God is another way of affirming the primal dignity of man as a creature in the divine image and as the object of God's love in the plan of redemption. This idea, drawing as it does upon the doctrines of creation and redemption, is pregnant with ethical and historical meaning. The meaning of human existence is expressed when man enters here and now into the relation of responsive and obedient love to God. In this act, he enters into the covenantal community of love into which God calls all men. Thus all social, political, economic, and cultural structures and processes of which he is a part are brought under the law of love. Every act of justice and every assessment of human rights becomes an expression of love.

Through the eyes of faith, Christians know that all men are equal. They know also from faith in creation that the individualities of men are real. But by means of their empirical experience, Christians know that men are unequal in gifts and cultural achievement—a concrete fact which is related to individuality. The knowledge of faith in equality, however, differs from the knowledge of inequality. Christians know that all men are equal, and there is no need to inquire as to who they are, who are equal; but, since Christians know that men are unequal in gifts and culture, they must always inquire as to who they are, who are unequal. Christian faith makes no decisions about inequality of capacity or skill until all men in a given situation have had an equal opportunity to try their capacities and skills. As T. V. Smith suggests, "the ideal of equality . . . means only this: Until we know who's who, we must treat men—especially treat children—as if they were equal, not because they are so, but in order to find out *who* is *who:* how unequal they really are." [15]

[15] Quoted in Weinberg and Shabat, eds., *Society and Man*, p. 264.

Men are the same and equal in their humanity. Since men are men, which is to say, centers of responsible decision, they are also the same and equal in their need for the opportunity to make responsible decisions. Owing to the individuality of their capacities, skills, and tendencies, the particular modes of their creative expression will differ widely. But "men equally have a right to full opportunity to do, each of them, what his life calls for, if it is to be lived successfully. No man has a greater right to full opportunity, nor a right to fuller opportunity than another man; and no man has less."[16] Equality of opportunity is logically and chronologically—since it must be applied to the children—the first plank in any concrete program of equality.

All aristocratic systems reject equality of opportunity, for all such systems understand man only in the mass. They do not know the individual. Among them, racism is the grossest violation of the reality of person. For racism alone melts individuals into a homogeny of being. When racism is in power, it describes the present power arrangements as reflections of superior human nature. Existent historic structures and existent social locations are believed to be natural and eternal. Since nature allegedly makes its essential divisions along racial lines, equality of opportunity among men can only be thought of as collectivistic.

God has created man as body, mind, and spirit in conjunction. These three dimensions of man always constitute an inseparable unity. No matter how physical a function to be performed may be, there is no way for a person to perform that function unless he brings his whole self along. For example, when the Brooklyn Dodgers first desegregated by bringing Jackie Robinson to the team, they were unable to provide Robinson with equality of opportunity. In all things physical and measurable, Robinson appeared to have equality of opportunity. He wore the same uniform and shoes as those worn by his teammates. He was free to choose a glove from the same range of possibilities. He used a bat of the same weight and length range, and "took his cuts" at baseballs over a plate that was seventeen inches wide just as the other players did. But he lacked equality of opportunity. He lacked equality of opportunity because he did not have equal access to the things of the mind and the spirit. He was exposed to race-baiting and isolation. He was not permitted to share the sense of belonging, comradeship, *esprit de corps*, stimulus, and hope. This state of affairs was soon reflected in his performance, and his batting average dropped to .227. Under ordinary conditions, he would have been sent back to

[16] Albert Hofstader, "The Career Open to Personality," in *Aspects of Human Equality*, Bryson *et al.*, eds., p. 121.

Montreal, but the Brooklyn front office had confidence in his ability and was determined to see him through the sociological jungle. Eventually, Pee Wee Reese put his arms around Robinson's shoulders at midfield in a gesture of good will and comradeship. Other players began to verbalize and display the we-consciousness, increasingly incorporating Robinson as a member of the team. Around the league he gradually became "another baseball player." As a person in developing community, Robinson went on to win Rookie of the Year honors.

Every truly human endeavor requires the whole person to perform it, whether it be the task of playing second base on a baseball team or pursuing graduate studies in a university. There is no equality of opportunity based on purely quantitative and measurable factors. Equality of opportunity is a right of persons and, therefore, must take into account the spiritual and psychological qualities of their beings as well as the physical. There can be no equality of opportunity that is not based on equality of whole persons. A Christian approach to equality of opportunity presupposes the equality of persons.

CHAPTER V

The Principal Plan of Political Action: Segregation

A. Why segregation?

THE logic of racism is genocide. Since in-races consider out-races defective in their humanity, there is no solution to the problem created by their presence in the world short of genocide. Spatial separation and quarantine on the earth are not enough. And when, at length, earthman enters into contact and interaction with men on other planets, if he or some members of the earth's population are still committed to the racist faith, spatial separation in the universe will not be enough. Defectiveness in the order of being can only be overcome by reversing the creation. Defective human beings must be exterminated. If it were possible for racist man, he would undoubtedly tamper with being as being. That is, he would uncreate out-races, for defectiveness in the order of being is deeper than defectiveness in the order of existence.

While genocide is the logic of racism, only one nation in history has ever made it an open and explicit national policy. Large numbers of members of out-races have been the victims of massacres from time to time, but the perpetrators of these evils were waging "limited war." The African slave trade was in effect a great episode in genocide, for probably three or four Africans perished under the brutality and inhumanity of the process for every one slave who landed on American shores. But in this case the objective was enslavement rather than genocide. It may be noted, however, that some Americans hoped and expected that the "Negro problem" would be solved by the death of the race after the abolition of slavery. This hope and expectation was based on the racist notion that the Negro race had not developed, nor was capable of developing, beyond the level of children. It was believed, therefore, that Negroes would be so dislocated psychologically under the conditions of freedom that they would be unable to fend for themselves and thus unable to survive. Despite this and similar extreme expressions of callousness, it was left to the Hitler regime in Germany to make genocide an objective of a national government.

The fact that genocide as a political plan of action has been so infrequent is undoubtedly due in part to the domestication of racism in Christian civilization. Although Christianity has allowed racism to grow and develop as a competing system of meaning and loyalty, it has nevertheless softened the brutalities of racial relationships. Perhaps Hitler is an illustration of what it takes to get the total solution adopted. That is, the total solution may be adopted at any time and in any place if an outright pagan dictatorship, inspired by the racist faith, seizes power.

But there is undoubtedly another reason why the total solution has been exceptional and that is sinful man's need to exalt himself and to dominate others. The history of mankind bears ample evidence that man is not satisfied with his God-given "dominion over the fish of the sea, and over the birds of the air, and over the cattle, and over all the earth, and over every creeping thing that creeps upon the earth" (GENESIS 1:26). Fallen man has an insatiable need to dominate man. His own sense of self-esteem rests upon lordship, not service. Even while making the claim to service, he honors that type of service which is exercised from a position of lordship.

For these reasons—and perhaps there are others—segregation evolved as the principal plan of political action in societies that implicitly believe in the elimination of the life of out-groups. Since the elimination of life is not feasible, the reduction of life becomes the working plan of action. Segregation is consistent with and inherent in racism because it is a part of a spectrum of belief on which extermination is the extreme point. Those who cannot bring themselves to exterminate depraved out-races can bring themselves to reduce their lives in the political communities of which they are a part.

B. The nature of segregation

Let us look into the nature of segregation to ascertain whether in fact it is a system which reduces life. Segregation may be defined as "the enforced separation of racial groups, either in regard to a few areas of life or in regard to many or all."[1] In the Southern United States the enforced separation of the races has traditionally been made in all areas of life.

In the definition of segregation, the word "enforced" must be given as much emphasis as the word "separation." Contrary to much popular opinion and especially the opinion of those who defend the system, segregation is not the expression of a social contract. It is not a covenant entered into by black and white people in a cool hour of reflection. It is not an agreement worked out in the interest of the smoothest possible functioning of society. Segregation is a hostile and contemptuous thrust of power by the strong. It is the product of a unilateral decision made by the dominant group alone, which aims precisely at the maintenance of an order of superordination and subordination.

Segregation is not inspired by a bad history of prior cruelties, oppressions, and exclusivistic systems imposed by the present out-race upon the present in-race. It is not inspired by a prior history of constant struggle between the two groups in which the one, then the other, was in a dominant position. By and large, racial segregation is practiced against those who have no history of perpetrating cruelty and inhumanity upon their present oppressors. If racism continues on earth, it does not follow that this will always be true; but up to the present time, the venom of racism is poured out largely on those who have been its historical victims.[2] This judgment includes anti-Mongolianism in the United States, for this form of racism did not have its origin in the war with Japan.

Segregation is born in hatred, fear, pride, and contempt. It knows nothing of love and does not aim at the general well-being; it is inspired by the spirit of pride and hostility, generated by the racist faith. Segregation is anticommunity. It is the structured will to deprive and reduce the life of the other. The appointed "place" of the other is *below*, and the functions of the other are the structured servilities of society.

Racial segregation must also be carefully distinguished from the various forms of voluntary segregation or separation that are functionally necessary in a complex society. A complex society is characterized by a multitude of tasks, many of which are institutionalized. The smooth execution of these various functions requires a degree of spatial

[1] Liston Pope, *The Kingdom beyond Caste* (New York, 1957), p. 80.

[2] The nationalistic forms of racism in Europe must be excepted. But the fullest expressions of racism have been imposed on the "nationally homeless"—Jews and Negroes.

separation. Those engaged in the teaching and learning process must draw apart from those who are manufacturing automobiles, in the interest of the undisturbed execution of activities peculiar to their respective objectives. Those who are worshiping must for that moment draw apart from those who are playing and enjoying a football game. And the two processes require permanently separate spaces, once they become institutionalized. The demands of concentrated attention make it necessary that most of life's tasks be spatially separated from tasks that are markedly different. But these voluntary acts of segregation for effective performance of task involve no invidious comparisons. They have nothing in common with racial segregation or any other segregation of persons as persons. Segregation for the performance of task means the separation of offices and of functionaries, not the separation of persons as such. In other words, this type of voluntary segregation does not involve the question of social distance. Social distance excludes or separates persons as persons.

Racial segregation is sometimes confused with the voluntary separation of national, ethnic, and linguistic groups in the early stages of their residence in a new political jurisdiction. Such groupings are quite normal and natural in that they represent the early efforts at adjustment and acculturation. At first, members of immigrant groups cannot speak the language of their new nation; they are poorly informed on the customs and patterns of behavior and generally do not know their way around. The voluntary ghettos thus serve as areas of schooling and adjustment. The older settlers of the first generation immigrants have become sufficiently enculturated in the new national culture to be able to stand in both the old and the new worlds. They are therefore ideal teachers for the newcomers who are about to begin the transition from the old world to the new. Once the newcomers have made the cultural adjustment, they tend to move out of their isolation voluntarily. Their original separation was never intended to be a permanent arrangement. It was a temporary mode of adjustment. It involved no judgments concerning their own worth or that of the natives of the new country. Except when immigrants are regarded as an out-race, once they depart from their voluntary separation, they are accepted by the majority group: they are absorbed in the main stream of the institutional and cultural life, and gradually improve their status in the society. This kind of voluntary and temporary segregation has nothing of the motive and purpose which constitute enforced and permanent racial segregation.

Frequently the issue of racial segregation is clouded by the defenders of the system who interpret segregation in such a way as to make it appear a fulfillment of the wishes of minority groups. Segregation is defended on the strength of such claims as: "they are happier among themselves"; "they are happier in their own churches"; and "98 per cent of the people of the South, white and black, want segregation." The last statement, of course, slips in a word about the wishes of the majority. Those who use this line of reasoning are seeking to establish normal, rational, and logical causes for the effects of the racist system.

In fact, however, the segregated areas of the cities of the United States are forced upon minority groups. The existence of the Negro church as Negro church is the result of the tearing asunder of the Body of Christ by the racist spirit. The originating and nurturing power of the Holy Spirit is boldly and unashamedly rejected. It is true that the Negro churches and the Harlems of the American cities have become islands of safety for many. They provide communities in which the daily symbols and experiences of inferiority can be avoided and self-respect can be affirmed. But this is only a partial victory. To the degree that segregation for protection from humiliation and from being set upon is the voluntary act of a minority, segregation is free from the enforcement of the majority. But it is not free from the prior enforcement of the majority and the continuous pressure of the hostile force of the majority.

> The great majority of the residents of Harlem cannot . . . avoid the fact that the very existence of Harlem as a separate community is largely a result of prejudice. They are still largely dependent upon white employers and white landlords. And even the internal structure and the processes of daily interaction within the segregated community are strongly influenced by the fact that it is a segregated area. This fact is always in the background, conditioning the internal status structure, influencing the nature of its leadership, affecting the cohesiveness of the community.[3]

Jewish communities, too, can be explained in part as instances of resort to the technique of avoidance. The individual Jew frequently finds his hopes of a nonprejudiced and nondiscriminating society shattered. The psychological effects of this experience are devastating. Consequently, he returns to the ghetto, not because he believes ghettos are good and desirable, but to avoid the continuous pressures of preju-

[3] George Eaton Simpson and J. Milton Yinger, *Racial and Cultural Minorities* (rev. ed.; New York, 1958), p. 234.

dice and discrimination for the sake of his own spiritual and psychological survival.

The voluntary segregation of the counter-racist Black Muslims also fails to disclose the genuine nature of racial segregation. Black Muslim separatism is the result of hostile, racist attitudes and power arrangements. Black Muslimism is a mythological and spiritually depraved reaction. Since the Black Muslims are without power, their separatism does not assume the nature of a political plan. They are unable to dominate and subordinate anyone. They simply separate themselves from the "white devils" and the "so-called Negroes" and become a community of self-help and mutual edification within the larger community. But they must depend on the larger community, economically, politically, and (in contradistinction to their own claims) even culturally.

Racial segregation is discrimination. It is "the differential treatment of individuals considered to belong to a particular social group." [4] Personal quality, merit, and achievement do not penetrate the consciousness of the racial segregationist. He directs his action against all members of particular ethnic groups without qualification and exception. The racial segregationist denies that there is any such thing as personal quality and merit in members of out-races, and he aims to limit their opportunity and achievement. Racial segregation is a political plan which refuses to take the individual into account at all. The individual simply does not exist in the racist consciousness. The racist believes that the segregation of an out-race is a natural way to deal with a human mass of perdition.

This idea was operating in a membership controversy that arose in a New Jersey Woman's Club. A Negro woman was nominated for membership in the club which was presumably dedicated to social welfare and cultural pursuits. The nomination was quite legal and in order, the nominator herself being a member of the club. But this particular nomination created a great deal of scurrying around on the part of the officers. A special cabinet meeting was called: past presidents were consulted. It was finally decided to reject the nomination. In reporting the decision to the member who put the name in nomination, the president said, "We all know Mrs. X; she is a fine person, a fine citizen, and a woman of lofty character, but—." The phrase which would have followed the conjunction was, of course, "she is a Negro." The nominator fell into tears, not because of the lot of the nominee but because of the spiritual condition of those who excluded her. She said, between

[4] Robin Williams, Jr., *The Reduction of Intergroup Tensions* (Washington: Social Science Research Council, 1947), p. 39.

her sobs, "I do so much wish you could find some taint of character, some acquired characteristic, which may be reproved in the nominee. But you are rejecting her on account of God's act, not her own. You exclude her solely on the ground of race. Her being and her being a Negro are inseparable. You therefore express offense at God's creative act."

When confronted by protests, the segregationist is fond of saying, "Let them earn their rights," or, "Let them improve themselves and then they can function as other Americans." But the fact is, segregationist barriers are erected as solidly against the opportunities for qualifying and improving the subordinated out-race as are the barriers against functioning after qualifying. As discrimination, segregation is a system which deprives all along the line of life. It does not merely deny the potential functionary opportunity to function because of the lack of qualifications. It aims to prevent his achieving qualification. Indeed, the segregationist is above all concerned with keeping the Negro deprived culturally as well as economically and politically because he fears that the Negro's history in America may yet correspond to that of European ethnic groups. The sons and daughters of European immigrant peasants have always been able to enter into the main stream of American life in proportions corresponding to their cultural improvement over their parents. But in the case of the Negro there has been, until recently, only the slightest correspondence between his cultural improvement and his participation in the main stream of American life. Only since World War II has there been evidence on a noticeable scale that the Negro would ever be permitted to have any part of the American dream. This small change which enhances the hope for a greater America in the hearts of some Americans is a challenge and a threat to the segregationists. It stimulates in them a revival and intensification of the call to action and vigilance lest the "sacred" segregated structure be lost.

Since racial segregation arranges people socially and politically according to the being which God has given them, it is inherently a permanent system and intends to be such. It aims to fix forever present disproportions of economic, political, and cultural participation on the part of races; and, in some cases, it aims to increase these disproportions. Racial segregation is enforced and permanent separation.

In addition to these two features of enforcement and permanence, racial segregation is characterized by superordination and subordination. The word "separation" in the definition of segregation does not mean that there is no intermingling of the races in a segregated society. There is in fact much intermingling. The closest contacts that Southern white people of status have had with persons outside the immediate family circle have been those with Negroes, both during the period of slavery and for the one hundred years since slavery. For the most part, Negroes have been the people who have ministered to their physical needs. Negroes have served white persons as cooks, waiters, maids, nurses, barbers, chauffeurs, butlers, confidants, and unofficial advisers. Segregation has not meant a strict spatial separation. The essential meaning of spatial separation is superordination and subordination. So long as the Negro accepts his lower-caste status, he has a great deal of freedom of movement and security. Thus, through the decades when no Negro could use a Pullman car as a passenger, he could use such facilities as a nurse or maid in the employ of white people. Ever since the Jim Crow laws and customs were established, Negro servants of white people have entered the public parks and other segregated places of the South as a matter of course. The spiritual and psychological dimension of this phenomenon is stated by Kyle Haselden:

> The Negro is required by the white man to "keep his place." But the Negro's place is not really a place but rather a manner and a mood; his "place" is spiritual rather than spatial. If his mood and manner are right, if his mood and manner reveal in him a genuine spirit of subjection, subordination, and dependency, then his place is almost anywhere. In such settings the physical nearness of the Negro is not abhorrent to the white man; all doors are open to him if he "knows his place." What is intolerable to the white man is the slightest suggestion on the part of the Negro that the Negro questions the fundamental and underlying assumption of his inferiority. When that happens, as it now does increasingly, the white man must substitute racial distance for racial doctrine in order to reassert his superiority. In a word, the Negro must be accepted on the white man's terms or be segregated from the white man.[5]

Segregation then is enforced and permanent separation typified by superordination and subordination. The appropriate "place" of an out-race is *below*. In the master-servant relationship, a Negro may occupy the same physical space as his white master, but the relationship itself

[5] Kyle Haselden, *The Racial Problem in Christian Perspective* (New York, 1959), pp. 134–135.

qualifies his space. The Negro's space is spiritually *below*. His spiritual beneathness must be symbolized in the arrangement of the physical spaces. If he lives in the same house, his room is a back room or is located in the basement. If his house is on the same lot, it is behind "the big house." This same psychology and spirit have historically been extended to public facilities and have made the doctrine of "separate but equal" as gross a fiction as was ever foisted on the American public.

From a Christian viewpoint, segregation not only denies the God-given dignity of man, it also violates the human oneness which God the Creator has established. Man is created for community. From the hand of God, man is for man. He is the covenant-partner of God and man. Racial segregation is immoral separateness. It denies God's created community and historic purpose for man, and introduces a politically enforced estrangement. But it goes beyond the actual practice of historical estrangement by declaring men to be enemies in their very being. Even an idolatry such as communism has not been so daring. Only in racism is the problem of existence rooted in the created being of large segments of humanity.

C. Justifications of segregation

The system of segregation is rationalized and supported by dogmas which constitute both a creed of faith and a charter for social conduct. These dogmas may be divided into two large classes—general justifications of the system and specific justifications for special places and functions.

The general and underlying justifications of segregation are propositions concerning nature, creation, being, and person. The claim is made repeatedly that the separation of the races belongs to the order of nature. The naturalness of segregation is sometimes simply asserted. At other times, it is referred to divine ordination. Segregation is also defended under such rubrics as "our sacred principles," and "the preservation of Christian ideals." But, above all, segregation must be preserved to prevent the "mongrelization" of the white race.

> If this [social desegregation] happens, then it will take an army of one hundred million men to compel it. We have through our forefathers, died before for our sacred principles. We can, if necessary, die again. You shall not show us how a white man "may

> go through the guts" of a negro! You shall not mongrelize our children and grandchildren.[6]

The executive secretary of the confederacy-wide Citizens Council Association, Robert "Tut" Patterson, speaks of segregation as the guardian of freedom and the bulwark against all forms of social and political evil as well as against "mongrelization":

> Integration represents darkness, regimentation, totalitarianism, communism and destruction. Segregation represents the freedom to choose one's associates, Americanism, state sovereignty, and the survival of the white race. These two ideologies are now engaged in mortal conflict and only one can survive. They cannot be fused any more than day can exist in night. The twilight of this great white nation would certainly follow. There is no middle ground.[7]

The naturalness of segregation is sometimes defended by reference to an instinct in the white man and a bodily condition of the Negro. It is said that white people have a natural aversion to the Negroes and, for this reason, cannot be expected to mix with them. At times, the idea of natural aversion is presented as a purely instinctive inner response. At other times, it is spoken of in connection with a stimulus which the Negro allegedly provides. The stimulus of the white man's aversion is said to be a very disagreeable body odor which is natural to the Negro. Less often, a segregationist claims that Negroes cannot tolerate the natural body odor of whites. The potency of the Negro body odor is described in the highest degree in the following report:

> A rabbi in a Georgia city, whose family has lived in the South for several generations, thought that this odor alone made separation worthwhile. He asserted that when walking along the street, "if a Negro had been that way fifteen minutes before, I can tell it." He added that he did not notice this in New York, nor with all the Negroes in the South.[8]

We have already observed that the psychology of primitive taboo does characterize the consciousness of many racists. It is verbalized in

[6] Tom Brady, *Black Monday;* quoted in James Graham Cook, *The Segregationists* (New York, 1962), p. 15.

[7] Quoted in Cook, *The Segregationists,* p. 65.

[8] Charles S. Johnson, *Patterns of Negro Segregation* (New York, 1943), p. 197.

such statements as "there is something about them that is repulsive to me," and "I feel that I would never like to touch one of them." To the racist, this "instinct" is a gift of nature. He does not understand that it is a "gift" of his culture. And he remains wholly unaware of the inconsistency between his experience of the feeling of racial taboo under conditions of equality, mutuality, and respect, and the absence of this feeling when he is dealing with the Negro "in his place." People who cannot bring themselves to shake hands with a Negro find no difficulty eating out of the hands of a Negro cook. His bodily odor is not annoying, if the Negro leans over a racist for the purpose of filling his plate with food. As already indicated, the most intimate contacts which the racist sustains, outside of the members of his own family, are likely to be with Negroes, especially in the South.

An equally serious fallacy in the doctrine that racial segregation is natural is the fact that it is first, last, and always a plan of political action. Those who justify segregation as a natural phenomenon are also the most vigorous supporters of segregation by law and public policy. They combine the argument from nature with the argument for law, without giving evidence of the slightest trace of awareness of the contradiction. The segregationist who is willing to trust the system to the workings of nature is yet to be found. It must be recalled that the naturalness of segregation is ascribed to the Negro also. It is said that both Negroes and whites accept it as natural. In effect, then, those who declare the naturalness of segregation are making a case for the elimination of segregationist laws although they remain unaware of this peculiarity in their thinking.

> They argue, for example, that since Negroes prefer to be together, as is evidenced to some degree by residential separation, in cities of the North where there is no legal segregation, segregation laws are justified. The defenders of the segregation pattern, who use the preceding argument, evidently fail to see one inconsistency in their reasoning. Really, if Negroes naturally prefer to be by themselves, why should anyone fear or oppose desegregation? If they would voluntarily maintain separation, what would any community or state lose, if it repealed its segregation laws? Voluntary separation would be a more logical argument for desegregation than for segregation.[9]

The justifications of segregation that are peculiar to Christian racists vary in the way they relate racism to Christianity. Christian

[9] T. B. Maston, *Segregation and Desegregation* (New York, 1959), p. 46.

racists relate racism to Christianity in two ways. The one is the way of assimilation; the other is the way of domestication. Many American Christians are so deeply committed to the racist faith that the power, promptings, and authority of the god of race are believed to be identical with the power, promptings, and authority of the God of biblical faith. For them it is the clear mandate of God himself that there should be racial segregation in every aspect of life. But for other Christian racists, perhaps more numerous, the racist faith is domesticated with the Christian faith. Devotion and service to the god of race are expressed *alongside* devotion and service to the God of biblical faith.

The degree to which racism is assimilated to Christian faith in America is not known. It is generally assumed that there is now considerably less assimilation of the two faiths than there was from the beginning of the period of agitation for abolition up to World War II, a period of about one hundred years. It is quite possible, however, that in the present racial crisis there is a tendency toward an increase in the assimilation of racism and Christianity. The rise of the White Citizens Council movement seems to be attended by a revival of claims that God himself is the author of segregation and the inspirer of prejudice. One and the same God, who is the source of life, love, and truth, our Savior from damnation, is also the source of hatred, pride, and falsehood, and the defender of oppression. Undoubtedly the most influential single tract of the present time, which elaborates the thesis that God and Jesus favor segregation, is an address by the late Rev. Dr. G. T. Gillespie. The address, "A Christian View on Segregation," was first delivered on November 4, 1954, before the Mississippi Synod of the Presbyterian Church. Since that time hundreds of thousands of reprints have been distributed by officers of the Citizens Council Association. It continues to be one of the most popular pieces of "educational literature" of the White Citizens Council movement.

Unlike many who have defended segregation as a clear biblical mandate, Gillespie concedes that his task is to draw valid inferences from biblical data:

> While the Bible contains no clear mandate for or against segregation as between the white and Negro races, it does furnish considerable data from which valid inferences may be drawn in support of the general principle of segregation as an important feature of the Divine purpose and providence through the ages.[10]

[10] G. T. Gillespie, *A Christian View on Segregation* (Greenwood, Miss., 1954, Educational Fund of the Citizens Councils), p. 8.

God's first act of separation was that of placing a mark upon Cain in order to distinguish his descendants from those of his brother Seth (cf. GENESIS 4:11–26). But eventually the descendants of Seth and Cain indulged in what Gillespie terms "promiscuous intermarriage," which "resulted in the complete breakdown of family life and such widespread immorality and wickedness as to provoke the Lord to destroy the earth with the flood" (cf. GENESIS 6:1–7).[11] A possible inference from this tragic story, and the one which Gillespie obviously favors, "is that the intermarriage of dissimilar groups, whether the differences be moral, cultural or physical, is not conducive to the preservation of wholesome family life or to morality, and therefore is contrary to the purpose and will of God." [12]

Genesis 9:18–29 furnishes the data for the third inference drawn from the Bible in support of the principle of segregation. The ninth chapter of Genesis contains the classic story for racist arguments. It was used as the primary biblical defense of slavery and ever since has been appealed to as the clearest mandate for the "places" of the racial groups. After the flood, Noah became "the first tiller of the soil." Having also planted a vineyard, on one occasion he overindulged in his own wine and fell into a drunken stupor. As Noah lay uncovered in his tent, Ham, the father of Canaan, saw him in this condition, but instead of covering his father, went out and told his brothers, Shem and Japheth. The two brothers brought a garment, and walking backward to avoid looking upon their father, covered his nakedness.

> When Noah awoke from his wine and knew what his youngest son had done to him, he said,
>
> "Cursed be Canaan;
> a slave of slaves, shall he be to his brothers."
> He also said,
> "Blessed by the Lord my God be Shem;
> and let Canaan be his slave.
> God enlarge Japheth,
> and let him dwell in the tents of Shem;
> and let Canaan be his slave."
>
> GENESIS 9:24–27

From this passage, Gillespie draws the traditional racist inferences. Since the sons of Noah are said to have overspread the whole earth,

[11] *Ibid.* [12] *Ibid.*, pp. 8–9.

Gillespie sends Shem to Asia, Japheth to Europe, and Ham to Africa, southern Asia, and the islands of the Pacific. The three sons are said to have become the progenitors of three distinct racial types in their respective places. The implications of these decisions and events for segregation are

> that an all-wise providence has "determined the times before appointed, and the bounds of their habitation." Which same providence by determining the climatic and other physical conditions under which many successive generations of the several racial groups should live, is thereby equally responsible for the distinct racial characteristics which seem to have become fixed in prehistoric times, and which are chiefly responsible for the segregation of racial groups across the centuries and in our time.[13]

Gillespie finds several other inferences in the Old Testament which support the principle of segregation but concedes that the New Testament is problematic as a source of biblical segregationist evidence. He strongly emphasizes the New Testament rebuke of Jewish intolerance, bigotry, and prejudice. But, since the New Testament does not demand revolutionary changes in the natural or social order, he asserts that "there would appear to be no reason for concluding that segregation is in conflict with the spirit and the teachings of Christ and the Apostles, and therefore un-Christian." [14] He concedes that "the redeeming love of Christ knows no limitations of class or condition or nationality or race," but he is confident that segregation is not in conflict with the spirit and teaching of Jesus because "he did not ignore or denounce racial distinctions nor did he set plans on foot to abolish them and to bring about amalgamation of the Jews and the Samaritans, or of any other races." [15]

Since Paul was the Apostle to the Gentiles, he naturally had more to say than other New Testament writers about the breaking down of the "wall of partition" between Jews and Gentiles. In his speech to the Greeks concerning God's creation of all nations of one blood and His determination of their habitation (ACTS 17:24–26), Paul, according to Gillespie, "affirms the unity of the race based upon a common origin concerning which there can be no difference of opinion among those who accept the authority of the Bible." [16] In his letter to the Colossians, the Apostle Paul affirms that "Here there cannot be Greek and

[13] *Ibid.*, p. 9. [14] *Ibid.*, p. 13. [15] *Ibid.*, p. 11. [16] *Ibid.*, p. 12.

Jew, circumcised and uncircumcised, barbarian, Scythian, slave, free man, but Christ is all, and in all" (COLOSSIANS 3:11). But Gillespie finds no moral guidance in this passage. He understands the passage as an affirmation of "the unity of all believers in Christ, regardless of their racial differences, but this unity is a spiritual relationship resulting from the mystical union of each believer with Christ Himself, in which all enjoy the same spiritual privileges and benefits."[17] At this point, Gillespie clinches his argument by referring again to the absence of any intent to wipe out racial distinctions:

> That Paul had in mind the absolute uniformity of believers in external relations and the wiping out of all distinctions of race, nationality, social status, sex or cultural heritage, is disproven by the fact that Paul never ceased to identify himself as a member of the Jewish race, and he made very practical use of his right to Roman citizenship.[18]

Although Gillespie believes that the Bible offers much support for the principle of segregation, he does not claim that this support comes in the form of a clear mandate; rather, he affirms that there is considerable biblical data from which inferences may be drawn. There are many segregationists, however, who are convinced that the Bible does provide a clear mandate in support of segregation. In their study of Christians in the Little Rock, Arkansas, crisis, Campbell and Pettigrew found much evidence of this conviction. One resolution passed by a church group will serve as representative of this type of theologizing:

> Whereas, in His infinite wisdom, for His eternal glory and for the good of man, God formed the various races of men upon the earth, separated them by geographical barriers, Acts 17:26, and encouraged their continued separation by differences in language, color, and other racial characteristics, GENESIS 10:5, 32; 11:1–9;
>
> Whereas God has never set aside his decree concerning the three sons of Noah and their descendants, Gen. 9:24–27, but has taught in the Bible that segregation of the races was and is His desire and plan, Israel being a notable example, especially in that God forbid the intermarrying of the Israelites with the black races of Canaan, GEN. 24:3–4, 28:1; DEUT. 7:1–3, 6; JOSHUA 23:12–13; EZRA 9:1–2, 10–12; I KINGS 8:53; and EXODUS 33:16.
>
> Whereas, being law-abiding citizens, as Baptists ever have been,

[17] *Ibid.* [18] *Ibid.*

> with a genuine love for humanity and the souls of men, regardless of race or color, having proved our loyalty by giving the blood of our sons to defend the laws of our country, having never practiced violence to force the beliefs of Baptists upon others, and consequently, being opposed to the use of physical force either to hinder or promote the integration of free men anywhere.
>
> Be it therefore resolved that we, the Arkansas Missionary Baptist Association, herewith voice our opposition to any force within or without our country, whether communistic, socialistic, or other, which seeks to destroy our democratic and American way of life; that we reaffirm our faith in the whole counsel of God's word; that we declare the integration of Negroes and Whites in our schools and society to be a threat to the security of our nation and contrary to the teachings of God both in the Bible and in nature; and that we hereby describe the Supreme Court rulings which favor integration of blacks and whites, and the uses of Federal troops to enforce those rulings, as being deplorable, unscriptural, and not in harmony with previous decisions of that body, nor with the beliefs and purposes of the God-fearing and democratic-minded men who at the first drafted the Constitution of the United States of America.[19]

Thus general justifications of segregation appeal to nature and to God's creative and redemptive purpose for the preservation of racial distinctions.

There is another class of justifications, specific for special places and functions. Specific justifications, of course, draw upon the general dogmas, but they are so formulated that they speak directly to a particular situation or the particular institutions or functions involved.

The Church is peculiar among all social institutions. It is the one institution on earth whose distinctive and essential mode of life and thought develop out of encounters with and responses to the Transcendent. The Church is the one historic institution which is definable in terms of the workings within its life of the Spirit from above. But for many American Christians, the god of race is authoritative for decision and action, even in the Church, when race relations are involved. An example of this is provided in the conversation of an upper-class white man and a bishop of a Southern area concerning the admission of a Negro to Church membership. The bishop resolved the issue, to his

[19] "Resolution on Integration," advertisement in *Arkansas Democrat* (Little Rock, Nov. 22, 1957, Arkansas Missionary Baptist Convention); quoted in Campbell and Pettigrew, *Christians in Racial Crisis* (Washington, D.C., 1959), p. 39.

own apparent satisfaction, by affirming the twofold nature of the Church and drawing the appropriate requirements from each. On the one hand, he declared, the Church is a divine institution. This imposes upon the congregation the requirement to accept the doctrine that all men are created equal and are equal in the divine plan of redemption. Evidently, the congregation is expected to accept this doctrine only in their minds. For the bishop goes on to say that since the Church is also a social institution, "Negro membership in a white church would be the opening wedge to social equality. If the races came together at a church meeting, there was no escaping social equality. Thus it was decided to reject the Negro membership." [20] Obviously, this means that the implications of the Church as a social institution are determinative where race is concerned, while the implications of the Church as a divine institution are accepted only intellectually. In short, the Body of Christ becomes merely an association of men, characterized by human sentiments, purposes, values, and even prejudices, when a person of an out-race seeks membership therein.

Group conflict always finds acute expression in the areas of scarce values. The economic life is accordingly a sphere of intense racial conflict, especially in matters pertaining to upgrading. In a caste society, segregation in the economic life takes the form of relegating the lower caste as a whole to the menial and undesirable tasks. This process, of course, must be supported by appropriate dogmas. Here as elsewhere, the foundation of any and all claims is the doctrine concerning natural being. Through the decades, the Negro in America has been relegated to menial and undesirable tasks because he is alleged to be naturally unfit for mechanical, technical, and clerical tasks, or for any type of complicated work. In the South, there is a tradition that the black Negro, sometimes known as a "buck nigger," is especially fitted for heavy work, but "must be driven to it like a mule." Several of the dogmas relevant to occupational segregation are expressed by the manager of a Louisiana oil company in an interview:

> The Negro is like a mule, a stolid sort of creature. He plods along, does his work well at his own speed, and doesn't wear himself out like the emotional white man. The southern nigger never worries about anything. Give him a full stomach and he is happy. I have worked all my life on a farm, and I envy him that. The Negro is too sluggish mentally for work in business. He just drifts along at a pace of his own. If you put him on a team he just lets them walk to town.

[20] Johnson, *op. cit.*, p. 189.

> Once in a while you get a good one as a mechanic on a truck, but they are exceptions. We have a lot of good Negro carpenters, brick masons, etc. Industry hasn't availed itself of the Negro to any degree. The Negro's mind doesn't act quickly enough. They are afraid of injuries, and that's expensive. Where they are employed in large numbers they hurt themselves. They are not mentally alert. We had a few working class white people. They had a deep seated prejudice against certain kinds of work; they like to have the Negroes do the menial things; they don't like to see white men do that. The Negroes make ideal servants; there are not better.[21]

The remark concerning the attitude and wishes of white workers suggests the clear intent to stratify the races occupationally. Often the Negro's natural unfittedness for occupational upgrading is asserted in conjunction with the declaration of white sentiment against his being upgraded. The belief prevails, however, that insofar as race is concerned, economic processes are organized by nature rather than history.

Until recent decades the social space of the Negro was so well defined in the South that residential segregation did not loom as an issue. This does not mean, however, that there was no live system of rationalizations to support this well-defined arrangement. It was assumed that the Negro quarters were "dirty, disease-laden, and dangerous." It was also believed that Negroes were "happier in their own neighborhoods." When Negroes began to appear in or near previously all-white neighborhoods, all the prevailing dogmas were used against them, plus the claim that "they depreciate property values since they do not keep up their property."

No controversy discloses the fact more clearly that racial exclusiveness involves the rejection of the fundamental being of members of outraces than the housing or space issue. The last generation has witnessed a great expansion of the Negro middle class. Many of these people have entered into the market in search for better housing. Character and cultural behavior are often not mentioned in the resulting housing controversies, except in the extremities of debate when a racist feels that he is obliged to say something else. The issue frequently focuses on the "loss of property values" exclusively, with no mention of the claim "since they do not keep up their property," because it is tacitly recognized that the Negroes in question will keep up their property. But

[21] *Ibid.*, p. 204.

Negroes, Jews, Japanese, etc., are nevertheless judged to be undesirable neighbors.

D. Desegregation and integration

In the field of race relations, American society is in a state of flux. Within the last decade, social change in this field has reached revolutionary proportions. Since American society is, and has been to a great degree, a color-caste society, the terms "desegregation" and "integration" are now in constant use. These terms belong together, but they do not mean the same thing. Desegregation refers to a process—the elimination of compulsory segregation. Desegregation may be voluntary or involuntary. It is voluntary when those who administer and make the policies of an institution freely decide to change its policy from one of racial exclusivism to one of racial inclusivism. It is involuntary when law, judicial decision, or public pressure requires such a change. Integration refers to a realized condition of community, involving mutuality, reciprocity, and respect among persons. Integration is voluntary and spiritual. The two terms belong together because in a racially segregated society, by and large, people of different racial groups lack the simple conditions and experience of togetherness upon which integration can exist without the prior process of desegregation.

Desegregation is referred to as a prior process because the mere "mixing" of the races is not integration. There is much desegregation in the United States outside the South but little integration. Integration requires more of persons than the mere removal of the external barriers and distances that separate them. But the transition from a segregated to an integrated society cannot be made without the process of removing the external barriers. The simple experiences of doing things together, such as working, playing, learning, etc., provide the foundation upon which genuine community can grow.

A society may be referred to as integrated when it has become a community of persons.

> In the deepest sense, integration has taken place only when those of another race or class are accepted as full and equal partners in a common task. It is based on mutual respect and on a sense of the dignity and worth of the human person.[22]

[22] Maston, *op. cit.*, p. 63.

An integrated society is one in which there is both a sense of and a will toward the common good. The common good is received through and communicated by persons. This means that an integrated society is one in which the individual person comes alive. It is not really the group which accepts or respects another group; it is, rather, a community of persons who accept and respect each other. In such a society, all definitions of function and opportunity presuppose the equal dignity of persons. Men are thus able in defining tasks to focus on those qualities of the individual person which are really related to performance; namely talent, training, knowledge, and skill. Extraneous issues, such as the question, "Who is your mother?" do not enter into the decision as to whether a man shall be permitted to study law in the state university. His admission to the law school rests on such criteria as his individual character, ability, and the quality of his prelegal training. And these are precisely the same criteria which every other person must individually meet in the society.

An integrated society in no sense reduces the individual. It is the one society in which a person can at all times be a person. In a racially segregated society, parochialism and prideful separation are normative values. Lest some people fail to interiorize these values, they are forced by law and custom to "keep step" in their external behavior. Thus a white man is required by law to relate to a Negro as a white man; he is not permitted to relate to him as a creature of God or as a religiously committed person. Obviously, the same law regulates the goings, comings, and doings of the Negro, except that it specifies that he remain "outside" or "beneath," in all matters pertaining to the larger society. To dare to act in a legally segregated society as a member of a more universal community of love than a racial community can provide is often to court imprisonment. An integrated society is, on the contrary, a community in which persons have become persons. They remain persons in all their relationships, for even professional and technical functions are exercised by persons.

The objection may rightly be raised that an authentic community of persons does not exist anywhere on a large scale; and accordingly, a truly integrated society, with or without a history of racial alienation, is an ideal. But to say this is not to dismiss such a society as a human and Christian requirement. Man never fully achieves any of his ideals that have the quality of the transcendent, but they are nevertheless incumbent upon him. In truth, an authentic community of persons would be a society of pure persons in which "the good of society and the good of each person would be one and the same good."[23] Although such a society is never fully realized, nevertheless it can be in process of realization if its ideal of the common good is informed and urged by that which transcends itself.

A society is integrated and is a genuine community of persons when it exists under God in fact. The community of persons is found in the common bond of the Spirit. The common good of society escapes every form of particularism—racial, class, religious, or otherwise—because the center of meaning and value transcends the society.

[23] Jacques Maritain, *The Person and the Common Good* (New York, 1947), p. 50.

CHAPTER VI

Racism and the Idea of Good and Evil

A. The notion of the good in racism

THE racist consciousness conceives of the good both as a quality of being and as a feature of conduct. The ultimate source of the good is nature. A man cannot really *be* good unless he possesses the right quality of natural being. He must have the genetic constitution of the superior race. A man can *do* good, who is a member of an inferior race, but he cannot *be* good. He cannot *be* good because he is defective in his humanity; but he can *do* good because conduct may be judged good or bad in the context of race relations. The racist consciousness judges conduct to be "good," "moral," or "right" which makes for the smooth working of the system of racial caste.

In racial relationships, good behavior for whites and Negroes is formally the same, but immensely different substantially. Since the relationship between Negroes and whites, particularly in the South, is a dominance-subservience structure and is unilaterally defined by the white man, the Negro is under greater strain than the white man to "keep the peace." A fundamental assumption of a caste system is that the condition which has been created by the power structure is a state of peace. Therefore peace can be and is only disturbed by the stirrings of the lower caste. The relationship between Negroes and whites in America, of course, had its beginnings in a master-servant arrangement. As the institution of slavery developed, it was assumed that it was a good, smooth-working, and natural relationship. Any conflict which arose during slavery was accordingly thought to be the exclusive creation of Negroes. Conflict during slavery was synonymous with the slave's getting out of his place.

In many circles today, the onus of keeping the peace rests on the Negro. The idea is verbalized in the oft-repeated statement, "If the Negro will but keep his place, our long-standing, harmonious, and peaceful race relations will be preserved." Even during the present period, when for the first time in American history protests have become widely accepted phenomena, if something goes wrong, it is the "Negro's cause" that is "set back." During the planning for the March on Washington, there were warnings from all quarters that the march should not be held because violence is inevitable owing to the sheer size of the gathering. Those who issued these warnings were for the most part agreed that the disturbances would not be precipitated by Negroes. But they were equally convinced that the onus would fall squarely upon the Negro who is seeking justice from *below* rather than upon those who actually caused the disturbance from *above*. Given the premises of the racist consciousness, the claim that peace must be maintained by the Negro alone is correct. If the caste system is just, if it is a reflection of the order of creation, if it is desired by those who have organized it, then the Negro and those whites who "have the temerity" to join him in seeking to change the system are destroyers of peace, justice, and well-being, no matter what means they may employ. But this very hypothesis reveals the sources of moral definition. The norms by which the racist consciousness judges race relations are drawn from the racist system. The racist can only take his stand within the circle of faith because the "mind of the idol" is in him.

When the Negro himself is spoken of as "good," the term refers exclusively to conduct; it does not refer to the depths of the inner life. The good Negro is "ole black Joe." He is the Negro who maintains "the proper attitude toward white people, and knows his place." On the other hand, a bad Negro is one who does not abide strictly by caste rules. He is not appropriately deferential in his behavior to white people. A normal show of self-respect is considered bad in a Negro. The very terms which are used to describe the bad Negro reflect the caste relationship. They are "sassy," "impudent," "uppity," and "trying to be like white folk."

The good Negro is often referred to as "humble," a term which has profound spiritual significance in the context of Christian faith. But when the racist consciousness applies it to the Negro, the term means manifesting a humblelike or deferential manner toward white people. Moral and spiritual terms applied to the Negro mean "manners" not "morals." The racist consciousness has no notion of morality in the life of the Negro in the fullest meaning of the word. The Negro is believed to be stationed somewhere between the beast and man in the order of being and, therefore, to be devoid of a genuinely human inner life. Accordingly, he does not and cannot interiorize moral norms and values. He cannot be educated or nurtured in high standards; he can only be "trained" after the fashion of a good horse. A good Negro then is one who has "good manners," having been "trained" in the context of the "right" racial relationships. He does not have "morals" because he is devoid of an inner life. His "morals" are "manners"; they are his behavior. This is what was meant above, when it was said, a member of an "inferior" race may do good, even though he cannot be good.

Since it is only in the context of racial relationships that his manners become significant, a good Negro may be notoriously immoral when judged by nonracist norms. The attitude which judges a Negro to be good solely on the ground of his fittedness within the caste system is expressed in a comment made by an interviewee to the authors of *Deep South:*

> Papa once had a Negro who was a big stout fellow, a fine worker and a good nigger around the whites. He was just as polite as could be and would do anything he was told. But he was Hell when he got out with the niggers. Papa first got him when defending him for killing another nigger. He got him off and he took up with papa. He later killed another nigger, and papa got him off again, but finally he killed a third and that was too much. He got fifteen years. However, all the white men said he was a good nigger, but they would admit he was a bad one among the other niggers.[1]

Unlike Negroes, Jews constitute an out-race at the competitive level. The Jew is not the man *below.* Everywhere in the world, he is a member of peer groups with anti-Semites. He is not an economically and culturally subordinated, second-class citizen. He enjoys the historical role of an equal, despite all the discriminatory irritations which he must face. But anti-Semitic literature appears to contain no concept of the "good Jew." To be good, members of out-races must be *below.*

[1] Allison Davis, B. B. Gardner, and Mary R. Gardner, *Deep South* (Chicago, 1941), p. 24.

They must have an appropriate space. Only in their "racially right" space can they exercise the "right conduct." Since modern history has failed to subordinate the Jew and thus provide him with an appropriate historical role, the Jew stands naked and exposed as a human disaster with no right to exist whatsoever. Even a Hitler might not have resorted to the "total solution" if the Jews were already a segregated group of second-class citizens all over Europe.

Since the Jew is a human disaster, whose life has not been properly reduced by segregation, he can do no good; but good can be done to him. That is, he can be destroyed. If the life of an out-race is not reduced by segregation, then the logic of racism must be applied; the out-race must be exterminated. A variation of extermination is exile. While exile does not remove an out-race from the earth, it does go beyond segregation by removing the out-race entirely from the space and presence of the in-race.

The idea that the compelling "good" is the destruction of a competitor out-race in the racist consciousness may be developed by comparing the revolutionary idea of the class struggle in Marxism with the Manichaeism of the anti-Semite. The Marxist is not opposed to the bourgeoisie in essence. There is a conflict of interests between them. The class struggle is not a conflict between good and evil; it is a struggle between sociohistorical groups. The aim of the revolutionary is accordingly to change the organization of society. The revolutionary adopts the point of view of the proletariat because it is he who is the victim of injustice and because Marx naïvely believed that this class possessed a culturally untainted perspective. Any member of the privileged class who supports the socialist cause is welcomed into the revolution. Although it is highly improbable that many of the bourgeoisie will support the revolution, this is due to the very situation of the privileged class rather than to some indefinable, interior demon which that class possesses. At any rate, those members of the privileged class who do break away and join the oppressed class will be judged by their deeds rather than by their essence.

> On the other hand, the Manichaean anti-Semite puts his emphasis on destruction. What he sees is not a conflict of interests but the damage which an evil power causes society. Therefore Good consists above all in the destruction of Evil. Underneath the bitterness of the anti-Semite is concealed the optimistic belief that harmony will be re-established of itself, once Evil is eliminated. His task is therefore purely negative; there is no question of building a new society, but only of purifying the one which exists. In the

> attainment of this goal the co-operation of Jews of good will would be useless and even fatal, and anyhow no Jew could be a man of good will. Knight-errant of the Good, the anti-Semite is a holy man. The Jew also is holy in his manner—holy like the untouchables, like savages under the interdict of a taboo. Thus the conflict is raised to a religious plane, and the end of the combat can be nothing other than a holy destruction.[2]

Further evidence that out-races cannot *do* good except in a position of subordination is seen in the counter-racist attitude of the Black Muslims toward the white man. In the Black Muslim lexicon there is no such thing as a good white man. In a sermon delivered in Atlanta, Georgia, Elijah Muhammed said, "There is no good in the white man. . . . All the whites are the children of the devil. We must separate ourselves as far as possible, for God did not intend for the two races to mix." [3] Since the white man has only been known as the "oppressor," the man who is *above*, no constructive historic role can be envisaged for him. Like the Jew in the anti-Semitic consciousness, the white man in the Black Muslim consciousness stands naked as a disaster in the order of humanity. A continuous annoyance to the Black Muslims are the "so-called Negroes" who find humanitarians, integrationists, and religiously committed men among the whites, and proceed to work with them for a Christian and democratic society. The "so-called Negroes" thus demonstrate how completely they have been "brainwashed." From the Black Muslim viewpoint, the white man always has evil intent in relation to the Negro. He always uses "tricknology" on the Negro. The white Christian, humanitarian, or integrationist is simply a super "tricknologist."

As an out-race without an appropriate historical role, the whites can do no good; but again, as in the case of the Jew, good can be done to them. They can be destroyed. In anti-Semitism, we have seen that destruction is the good when an out-race is on equal terms with the in-race. Now we see that racism must also rely on destruction when it finds itself below. At the present stage in history, the strategy of the Black Muslims calls for separation from the white man "as far as possible." Their low social, political, and economic position and their extremely limited resources make a program of destruction impossible.

[2] Jean-Paul Sartre, *Anti-Semite and Jew,* trans. George J. Becker (New York, 1960), p. 43.

[3] Quoted in James Graham Cook, *The Segregationists* (New York, 1962), p. 337.

They must therefore resort to apocalyptic hopes and expectations. They look forward to the doom of the white man which Allah has promised and will bring to pass about 1984.

B. The racist ethic of race relations

The issue of justice, equality, and human dignity is clouded over and over again in American Negro-white relations by the repeated racist claim that race relations are already peaceful, harmonious, and just. The American public is warned that all civil rights efforts are the work of either agitators, communists, or the "power-hungry" federal government. The relations between "our white and colored citizens were just fine until these outside agitators began their disturbances."

Those who develop this line of thought point to the great progress of the Negro in America. Forgetting for the moment all of the things which they otherwise say about the Negro's limitations and lack of potential, they hail his progress as an achievement in one century that is unique in the history of mankind. The Negro's progress is used to prove the unequaled friendliness and helpfulness which the white man has extended to him. The fact that the Negro is inadvertently being given credit for taking creative advantage of opportunities is entirely overlooked. Usually there is the added claim that the Negro himself likes the system, always has, and would never part with it, were he not "stirred up" by "outside agitators."

These claims can only be properly understood when they are viewed in the racist perspective. We have already seen that the idea of the good for the racist consciousness is a norm drawn from the racist faith. Similarly, "good race relations" are racistically defined. Since there is no historic role for an out-race to play except in a position below, it follows that only the system of racial castes can constitute good race relations. When a racist then proclaims "fine, peaceful, and harmonious race relations," he is declaring his joy and satisfaction in the caste system. The following statement by the author of *Black Monday* may be taken as a classic presentation of racist paternalism.

> If you had a negro mammy take care of you and keep you from eating dirt; if you played with negro boys when a boy; if you have worked with and among them, laughed at their ribald humor; if you have been stunned by their abysmal vulgarity and profanity; if you can find it in your heart to overlook their obscenity and depravity; if you can respect and love their deep religious fervor; if you can

> cherish their loyalty and devotion to you, then you are beginning to understand the negro.
>
> If you have had a negro man and his wife and children live and work with you on your place; if he has worked your crops, tended your cattle, and performed all other obligations; if his wife has cooked your meals, cleaned your house, and watched over your children; and you, in turn, have fed and clothed all of them and protected them from anyone who would harm them; if you bought the school books for their children; if you have paid the installments on the car which they own, permitted them to use your gas and oil; if you have bailed the husband out of jail on Monday morning after his "crabapple switch" had been too active in a dice game or at some "tunk" on Saturday night; if you have taken him to the doctor and had his wounds treated, paid his bill and fine without expecting to be or having been reimbursed; if, when his wife or one of his little children becomes ill, you provided the best medical care possible without any cost to him because of the friendship which existed between you, and if death struck his little one, you grieved with him and you bought and gave the coffin to him, in honor of the dead, because of the affection which exists between you; if you have given him, in addition to his salary, extra money at Christmas and at other times in order that he might buy some presents for the three or four illegitimate children which he acknowledges as his own, then you are beginning to know the negro and understand his problems.[4]

It is clear from this account that not a single adult decision is left to the Negro father and husband himself. It is also clear that Brady is convinced that he is describing every Negro on God's earth; and somehow all these traits, even those which contradict each other, are rolled together in every Negro. It is also obvious that the relationship described is but a step removed from slavery. But for Brady, it is the system in which the Negro can best be himself and live and move in "appropriate community" with the white man.

Of course the paternalistic system is not so complete and thorough as Brady describes in every setting in which a racist is in command. But Brady has described the "ideal." The ideal continues to be the structure of relationships of the plantation civilization. Even so delicate and intimate a matter as eating may be engaged in with the out-race Negro under the appropriate conditions. Roy V. Harris, publisher of the white supremacist *Augusta Courier*, national president of the Association of Citizens Councils of America, and president of the Georgia

[4] *Ibid.*, pp. 24–25.

States' Rights Council, sought zealously to convince an interviewer that he felt no ill will whatsoever toward Negroes. To give concreteness to his contention, he said, "Many times I've sat under a cotton patch tree with Negroes and eaten together with them." [5] But Harris hastens to add that "he and his fellow cotton pickers, the Negroes, never did quite mix—not in the manner recommended by the NAACP anyway." [6] Harris means that the NAACP is seeking to mix the races "socially"; but under the cotton patch tree, even though there was a common meal, the lines of the racist caste system were duly recognized and symbolized.

That Harris should credit himself with harboring no ill will toward the Negro despite his associations and long racist political record in Georgia may be described as a massive piece of self-deception. But it is the self-deception that is inherent in Christian racism. The claim that "I act with no ill feelings" toward the Negro or "this is not prejudice" is a frequent cry of Christian racists. The Christian racist, like his pagan racist brother, is impelled inevitably to political action that is directed *against* out-races; but he views this as a *natural* fact of life. Such action belongs to the natural order of being. This is what the unashamed pagan racist philosophers have said; but they do not hesitate to admit that which the Christian racist cannot admit—namely, the belief that life is inherently a fight and a struggle.

Christians as Christians find it exceedingly difficult to admit the presence of pride and hatred in their own hearts. Through the centuries, Christianity has taught that pride is the chief of sins and that "pride goes before destruction, and a haughty spirit before a fall" (PROVERBS 16:18). Christians who practice the polytheism of simultaneous adherence to the God of the biblical faith and to the idol of race frequently require in themselves the purgative of verbalization, as a self-deceptive release from guilt. They do in fact hate and detest the Negro and oppress him. But these evil spiritual traits and habits must in some way be exorcised from their "Christian life." They are accordingly transmuted verbally. Unless the idolatrous racist faith itself is overcome, there can be no change in fact. But the Christian racist can be "released" for action by a simple play on words.

The pronouncements of Herbert Ravenel Sass, a South Carolinian, an independent, and an Episcopalian, constitute an excellent illustration of how sin is purged verbally from racial prejudice and discrimination. Sass admits that prejudice is at least irrational, so he simply denies its presence in racist motivation and substitutes the idea of "race preference."

[5] *Ibid.*, p. 102. [6] *Ibid.*

> Between prejudice and preference there is vast difference. Prejudice is a preconceived unfavorable judgment or feeling without sound basis. Preference is a natural reaction to facts and conditions observed or experienced, and through the action of heredity generation after generation it becomes instinctive. Like separateness, it exists throughout the animal kingdom. Though the difference between two races of an animal species may be so slight that only a specialist can differentiate between them, the individuals of one race prefer as a rule to associate with other individuals of that race.[7]

Sass goes on to point out that the founders of this country—people of British, German, Dutch, and Scandinavian stock—were imbued with the instinct of race preference. In this sense, they must be contrasted with the founders of South and Central America, who amalgamated with Indians and, in some cases, with Negroes. On the strength of this observation, Sass concludes that it is nonsense to speak of racial discrimination, "the necessary consequence of race preference," as "un-American." [8] Rather, racial discrimination is the most distinctively American thing. The nation is built solidly upon it. It makes the American people what they are.

At this point, Sass feels called upon to add that racial discrimination also is devoid of evil. He admits that there are types and degrees of racial discrimination that are bad—"outdated relics of an earlier time when conditions were unlike those of today, and these should be, and were being, abolished until the unprecedented decree of the Supreme Court in the school cases halted all progress." [9] But the term "discrimination" as usually employed is a misused word. "It does not necessarily imply either stupidity or sin. It is not a synonym for injustice, and it is very far from being, as many seem to think, a synonym for hatred." [10] While the Southern white man has always exercised discrimination in regard to the Negro, he has never hated him, except in a few untypical cases, says Sass. He also bears testimony that this has certainly been the case with himself and with other white people in the old plantation region of the South Carolina low country, where he has spent his life.

> What does exist strongly and ineradicably, is race preference. . . . This preference should not and in fact cannot be eliminated. It is much bigger than we are, a far greater thing than our racial dilemma. It is—and here is another basic fact of great significance—an essential element in Nature's huge and complex mechanism.[11]

[7] Herbert Ravenel Sass, *Mixed Schools and Mixed Blood* (Greenwood, Miss., 1956, Educational Fund of the Citizens Councils), p. 4.

[8] *Ibid.*, p. 5. [9] *Ibid.* [10] *Ibid.* [11] *Ibid.*, p. 6.

Thus we see again how pressing is the need in the racist to understand himself from below. He is a child of nature. Even if he claims to be a child of God, in the context of race relations, he understands himself naturalistically. He is a person urged by an instinct, the "instinct of race preference." Discrimination is allegedly the *necessary* consequence of race preference. Racist man is not a free responsible spirit; he is not even a rational being; he is a necessitated being belonging to the order of nature. Therefore, in the context of his faith, he is convinced of the rightness of what he does because his attitudes and actions are necessitated. His life must be understood in terms of "blood" and vital impulses. It cannot be understood in terms of reason and spirit. But, what is worse, as a racist he remains unaware of the fact that he views himself solely as a child of nature.

The ethic of race relations to which the counter-racist Black Muslims commit themselves is governed by two principles, "separation," and the "law of retaliation." The great distance of the white man from the black man in the order of being makes him an incorrigible enemy of the black man. "Islam sent several prophets, including Moses and Jesus, to offer Islam to the white man as a religion of brotherhood. But the white man could not accept it, for the white race is evil by nature and cannot love anyone who is not white." [12] The advice which is deemed appropriate to this claim is separation from the white man as much as possible.

The Black Muslims also advise separation for a historical reason. It is the only way that the black man can ever gain self-identity and proceed to develop himself on the strength of that self-identity. The so-called Negro in America cannot find himself because he is the victim of the "looking-glass view" of himself. He sees himself through the eyes of the white man. This is a "manipulated" image. The separated Black Muslim community presumably provides an experience and a tradition in which genuine self-knowledge and self-improvement are possible.

Black Muslims are advised by their teachers never to bother anyone. They must never be the cause of a disturbance. But if the natural enemy, the white man, molests them, they are to retaliate. Not only is this line of conduct right because the white man is the natural enemy, it is also right because it is the divine law. If Jesus had permitted Peter and the other disciples to employ it, He might have been more successful in his work. God has made provisions throughout nature for every creature to protect himself against his enemies. The black Christian preacher lies about this, having permitted himself to become the white

[12] C. Eric Lincoln, *Black Muslims in America* (Boston, 1961), p. 78.

man's most effective tool in the pacification and control of the so-called Negroes.

The law of retaliation is also proclaimed as the only alternative against injustice. The Christian government in America is no defense against the injustice perpetrated on the black man. Not even the Pope in Rome can do anything about it. "If you and I don't wake up to that knowledge and execute the law of an eye for an eye, we might as well be dead and forgotten." [13] Malcolm X adds that the law of retaliation is the only thing that will impress the white man. It is the law which the white man himself uses; and it is the only thing that will make the black man respected over the earth.

C. The fall and sin in racism

In the racist doctrinal system, the fall occurs whenever a superior, conquering race mixes its blood with the "lower" races it has conquered. The fall is the degradation of pure human being by means of the infiltration of the genes of defective human being into the gene pool of the former. It is an occurrence in the "history" of nature. But since that which is natural is the fundamental and essential, since the genetic mechanism is the ground and determination of the rational and spiritual life, the loss of racial purity is total loss and therefore fall. The mixing of the "blood" of a superior race with that of an inferior race is a loss of such proportions that nothing can compensate for it and no new thrust of life can spring from the wreckage.

> Everything in the world can be improved. Any defeat can become the father of a later victory. Any lost war can become the cause of a later rise, every distress the fertilization of human energy, and from every suppression can come the forces of a new spiritual rebirth, as long as the blood remains preserved in purity. Alone the loss of the purity of blood destroys the inner happiness forever; it eternally lowers man, and never again can its consequences be removed from body and mind.[14]

> Whenever and wherever the white man has drunk the cup of black hemlock, whenever and wherever his blood has been infused with the blood of the negro, the white man, his intellect and his culture have died. It is as true as two plus two equals four.[15]

[13] *Ibid.*, pp. 186–187.

[14] Adolf Hitler, *Mein Kampf* (New York, 1940), p. 452.

[15] Brady, *Black Monday,* quoted in Cook, *The Segregationists*, p. 17.

Students of history and anthropology are well aware that the mixing of races is a perennial phenomenon; but when the sweeping generalization is made that race mixture has destroyed civilizations, they are at a loss in the search for specific instances. In an essay entitled "The Kiss of Death," John W. Hamilton and his Citizens' Protective Association of St. Louis claim to provide the answer. In this essay, the mixing of the races is presented as a Russian program, dedicated to the destruction of America.

> We look frantically around for Russian spies, believing that Russia will attack us with armies. . . . In the meantime Russia is laughing. She has a more deadly weapon than the atomic bomb. She knows our strength is in our white stock and that when she has mixed our blood with Negro that we are licked forever. . . .
>
> Negro blood destroyed the civilization of Egypt, India, Phoenicia, Carthage, Greece, and Rome. . . .
>
> Remember, mixing white children with Negroes is a form of insanity. It takes the form of religion, democracy, brotherhood, etc. It is a pollution complex directed from Moscow. Remember discrimination is not a sin. It is a sign of Mind or God working through man to protect what is good.[16]

"Racial impoverishment is the plague of civilization," writes Stoddard.[17] It occurs and recurs. It is a "hideous disease" and like a consuming fire has reduced "the proudest societies to charred and squalid ruin."[18] An illustration of this recurring phenomenon is provided by Adolf Hitler. Aryan tribes, often in very small numbers, move in and subjugate foreign peoples. Stimulated by the favorable factors of fertility, climatic conditions, etc., in the new territory, and favored by a mass of subject and inferior people at their disposal, "they develop the mental and organizatory abilities, slumbering in them."[19] In the course of time, they create cultures which express their own inner character, adapted to the new territorial environment and the subject people. "Finally, however, the conquerors deviate from the purity of their blood which they maintained originally, they begin to mix with the subjected inhabitants and thus they end their own existence; for the fall of man in Paradise has always been followed by expulsion from it."[20]

A strange pessimism runs through the racist philosophy. Not only

[16] Quoted in Cook, *op. cit.*, p. 59.

[17] Lothrop Stoddard, *The Revolt against Civilization* (New York, 1922), p. 88.

[18] *Ibid.* [19] Hitler, *Mein Kampf*, p. 400. [20] *Ibid.*

have the superior races fallen with their proud civilizations through the millennia, but they do and will continue to fall. Every great conquest and period of creative achievement is followed by a fall. If the premise of the racist concerning human nature is accepted, explanation as to why the fall should occur is impossible. The superior race is alleged to be intrinsically good and wise. Its power is an inner resource, based on its given nature. Wisdom and virtue have their ground in the natural being of the superior race. No environmental or historical factors in themselves can ever affect the virtue of superior men. But this one thing superior races lack: they lack the endowment of wisdom and virtue equal to the choices necessary for remaining superior. At this point, the racist ideologists are involved in a greater puzzle than even the communists. As is the case with many utopian formulations, Marxism has elaborated a doctrine of primitivism, an original communist stage in the history of mankind from which the present communist movement may draw its models of the classless society. But Marxism cannot explain the very "problem of history" which is its concern. The Marxists cannot tell us why a stage of pure communism should ever degenerate and be lost. Perplexity is even greater for racism inasmuch as the racist ideology claims the fall of once-perfect human beings, rather than once-perfect social structures. Communist explanations of virtue and wisdom are at least in historical terms, despite their trouble with the beginning and end of history. But the racist ascribes a natural endowment to superior races, and rejects adamantly all explanations of environmentalism.

Against the background of the declaration that civilization depends absolutely upon quality, and quality upon inheritance; and after making the ultimate claim that "given a high-type stock producing an adequate quota of superior individuals . . . a civilization might be immortal,"[21] Lothrop Stoddard offers an explanation as to why civilizations do in fact decay. Three destructive tendencies, sooner or later, bring civilizations to decline and ruin. They are: "(1) the tendency to structural overloading; (2) the tendency to biological regression; (3) the tendency to atavistic revolt. Here are the three grim Nemeses that have dogged the footsteps of the most promising peoples."[22]

Structural overloading means that the increasingly massive and complex superstructure of civilization becomes too heavy for an inherited and constant human capacity to bear. In the development of civilization, each succeeding generation further elaborates the social environment, and leaves a permanent deposit of cultural material. Since

[21] Stoddard, *The Revolt against Civilization*, p. 11. [22] *Ibid.*

social acquisitions cannot be taken over except at great cost in mental labor, sooner or later a point is reached where many individuals cannot scale the mountainous heights of the accumulated body of knowledge. When the number of such individuals becomes a large proportion of the society, the social regression of the entire society or the decline of civilization has occurred. This process is inevitable in every high civilization because the civilization may be elaborated endlessly, but human capacity remains virtually constant or declines. During the entire historic period, mankind, including the highest human types, has made no perceptible biological advance.

If this mechanical influence were the only one which civilization exerts on its bearers, matters would be serious enough; but in addition to this, civilization exerts profoundly significant influences on its bearers. Unfortunately, these are mainly of a destructive character. "The stern truth of the matter is that civilization tends to impair the innate qualities of its human bearers; to use up strong stocks; to unmake those very racial values which first enabled a people to undertake its civilizing task." [23] In short, biological regression sets in.

Prior to the advent of civilization the human species underwent profound differentiations, both between separate races and within the various stocks. "Age after age, nature imposed upon man her individually stern but racially beneficent will, eliminating the weak, and preserving and multiplying the strong." [24] Eventually the gifted races began to create civilizations. Civilization wrought the change from natural selection to social selection. But the effect of social selection on survival values was negative all along the line. On the one hand, it enabled large numbers of weak, degenerate, and stupid people to live and beget children. On the other, its effect on the strong was to induce them to have fewer children, even though "the strong individual survived even better than before." [25] Reproduction was lessened among the superior because "civilization opened up to them a whole new range of opportunities and responsibilities." [26]

In the altered situation which the plane of civilization provides

> the successful superiors . . . were alike allured and constrained by a host of novel influences, power, wealth, luxury, leisure, art, science, learning, government—these and many other matters increasingly complicated life. And, good or bad, temptations or responsibilities, they all had this in common: they tended to divert human energy from racial ends to individual and social ends.[27]

[23] *Ibid.*, p. 16. [24] *Ibid.*, p. 17. [25] *Ibid.* [26] *Ibid.*, pp. 17–18.
[27] *Ibid.*, p. 18.

Absorption in personal and social matters induced the successful superiors to marry late, have fewer children, and even to practice celibacy. These factors combined to thin the ranks of the superior and improverish the race. Meanwhile, the inferior, no longer weeded out by natural selection, increased and multiplied. This process of biological regression has blighted all civilizations.

This account of biological regression is a glaring contradiction of Stoddard's central racist claim that the quality of persons and civilizations is determined by the germ-plasm alone. Here he admits that the superior race is "allured and constrained by a host of novel influences." He has also said that "civilization tends to impair the innate qualities of its human bearers; to use up strong stocks, to unmake those very racial values which first enabled a people to undertake its civilizing task." Such statements and admissions do not square with the claim that the germ-plasm is "carefully isolated and protected against external influences," and "persistently follows its predetermined course." [28] They are also discordant with the judgment that environmental influences are of no or extremely little importance in the development or deterioration of man. "Biological regression" is palpably a result of cultural influences. The civilization which "superior man" creates becomes a Frankensteinian monster which destroys him. At the moment of its greatest height, the superior race lacks the innate quality equal to the task of sustaining itself.

The influence of history and culture may also be seen in Stoddard's explication of the tendency to atavistic revolt. Broadly speaking, he asserts, society may be divided into three classes—superiors, inferiors, and intermediates. These classes shade imperceptibly into each other; between them are intermediate zones composed of "borderline" individuals. Progress is due primarily to the superiors, but "most of the intermediate grades are near enough to the superiors to understand and assimilate what the superiors have initiated." [29] But the inferior elements are uncivilizable and therefore instinctively the enemies of civilization.

The word "inferior" applies to all those people in a society who are below or beneath the standard of civilization. The category includes primitives—congenital savages or barbarians, men who could not fit into any civilization—and degenerates, that is, the imbecilic, feebleminded, neurotic, and insane. "Moreover, besides primitives and degenerates, civilization by its very advance automatically condemns fresh multitudes to the ranks of the inferior." [30] Many individuals who

[28] *Ibid.*, p. 44. [29] *Ibid.*, p. 21. [30] *Ibid.*, p. 22.

effectively accommodate to early phases of civilization do not possess the mental and moral fiber to stand the sterner tests of higher and more complex civilizations. The discipline and burden of civilization oppresses the inferior or "Under-Man." In addition to his innate handicaps, his weaknesses and incapacities are exploited by better-placed individuals, and he is driven to social levels lower than those dictated by his natural capacity. Thus social discontent is added to the basic attitude of Under-Man, which "is an instinctive and natural revolt against civilization. . . . Every society engenders within itself hordes of savages and barbarians ripe for revolt and ever ready to pour forth and destroy." [31]

"When a civilization falters beneath its own weight and by the decay of its human foundations; when its structure is shaken by the storms of war, dissension or calamity; then the long repressed forces of atavistic revolt gather themselves together for a spring." [32] The noteworthy fact in the appearance of revolt is that the leaders are able men. The revolutionary officers' corps is composed of the "borderliner," the "disinherited," and the "misguided superior."

The borderliner turns against society because he cannot quite make good. The disinherited is incapable of civilized success, but is also a victim of social injustice or individual wrongdoing. Some of the disinherited possess marked talents and are therefore very dangerous enemies. The misguided superior is the strangest phenomenon. "As the Under-Man revolts because civilization is so far ahead of him, so the misguided superior revolts because it is so far behind." [33] The misguided superior ascribes his own lofty impulses to mankind. He dreams of short cuts to the millennium, failing to realize that the goals of the forces of social revolt are profoundly different from his own. When he understands the unmasked face of barbarism, it is too late. He is trampled in the mud.

When the social revolution is in full swing, society falls into the grip of its barbarians, and

> every individual falls more or less under the sway of his lower instincts. For, in this respect, the individual is like society. Each of us has within him an "Under-Man," that primitive animality which is the heritage of our human, and even our prehuman, past. . . . This primitive animality, potentially present even in the noblest natures, continuously dominates the lower social strata, especially the pauper, criminal, and degenerate elements—civilization's "inner

[31] *Ibid.*, p. 24. [32] *Ibid.*, p. 25. [33] *Ibid.*, p. 26.

> barbarians." Now, when society's dregs boil to the top, a similar process takes place in individuals, to whatever social level they may belong. In virtually every member of the community there is a distinct resurgence of the brute and the savage and the atavistic trend thus becomes practically universal.[34]

Thus Stoddard takes away with one hand that which he has given with the other. His primary claim is the ultimacy of the superior race. He is so daring he can even say, "given a high-type stock producing an adequate quota of superior individuals, and a civilization might be immortal." [35] Yet, in the explication of the tendency to atavistic revolt, he admits the presence of the brute and the savage in the nature of the superior race, and shows how these tendencies are evoked by sociocultural conditions. Stoddard's elaborate efforts to account for the decay of civilization on racial grounds end in a disproof of his thesis. His own explications as to why the inherently wise and virtuous freely abandon their historic and creative task call into question the very inner quality which has been ascribed to them.

The meaning of sin is apparent in the discussion of the fall. Sin is a particular expression of primal sin or the fall. To the racist it is any and every act of race-mixing. Race-mixing is a sin against the will of the Eternal Creator.[36] It leads to the doom of man because in the act of race-mixing, man is trying to resist "the iron logic of Nature and thus becomes entangled in a fight against the principles to which alone he, too, owes his existence as a human being." [37]

Hitler deplores the fact that the Old Reich failed to give attention to the question of the preservation of the racial foundations of nationality. The racial foundations of nationality constitute the sole right which gives life in the world. If a people do not respect their racial foundations, they have no right to complain about the loss of their worldly existence. "Peoples which bastardize themselves, or permit themselves to be bastardized, sin against the will of the eternal Providence, and their ruin by the hand of a stronger nation is consequently not an injustice that is done to them, but only the restoration of a right." [38]

In the United States, micegenation is the racial sin. Interestingly enough the term "miscegenation" is mainly an American word. It is an emotionally loaded term and is used almost exclusively to denote sexual relations between Negroes and whites. Miscegenation is said to be

[34] *Ibid.*, p. 27. [35] *Ibid.*, p. 11. [36] Hitler, *Mein Kampf*, p. 392.
[37] *Ibid.*, pp. 392–393. [38] *Ibid.*, p. 452.

"contrary to nature," "detestable," and "contrary to human instincts." Even Christian monogamic marriage between white and Negro persons falls under the opprobrium of miscegenation.

Despite the claim that miscegenation is contrary to nature, detestable and contrary to human instincts, the preservation of the "purity of the white race" is not left to nature's designs. Rather, it is assumed that there must be "eternal vigilance" and the support of the whole cultural apparatus to maintain racial purity. Thus race-mixing is not the sole evil, even though it is the primary one. Other evils are whatever relationships between the races that might lead to the mixing of the races. "Social equality" is the common term for racial sin. The meaning of social equality is vague and elusive, but this has a political advantage. While intermarriage is the kernel idea, the nonspecific fear of social equality can be and is used to inspire efforts to preserve the caste order all along the line. Fanatical racists fear that even "if you give the Negro the vote, he will marry your daughter." Accordingly the specter of that all-encompassing evil, social equality, is conjured up to inspire opposition to and fear of every conceivable change in the caste order, including the most impersonal forms of human existence. Thus programs of simple justice are believed to be the designs of communists, agitators, outsiders, and evil men who "would destroy our sacred way of life."

In the counter-racism of the Black Muslims, sin is the spoiled, poisoned, and brainwashed condition of the American Negro—the Lost Nation of Islam in North America. It is, of course, the white man who has perpetrated this evil upon him. The most unforgivable sin of the so-called Negroes is the fact that they love the white race. Fortunately for the Negro, "Allah is not unforgiving, and the sins of the Lost Nation committed in following and obeying the Slavemasters are not held against them if they return to their own kind." [39]

D. The racist transformation of Christian values

In the main, the devotees of the racist faith have been Christians and citizens of Christian civilization. The relationship of racist morality to Christian morality has therefore been a persistent problem. The racist ideology was born out of the conditions of imperialism and slavery. The human relationship which this ideology originally justified was one of extreme dominance and subservience. In the earliest days of

[39] Lincoln, *op. cit.*, p. 74.

contact, the master group was constituted of Christians while the slaves and natives were heathens. In time the rudiments of the Christian faith were extended to the subordinate groups, but with the advent of modern secular imperialism and slavery, even Christian baptism could not change the status of imperialized or enslaved subordinates.

The Christian master race has never been content to relate itself to subject races solely on the strength of the pagan justifications of a racist ideology, even though its relationship to subject races was guided primarily by racist ideas and values. It was necessary, therefore, to bring Christian norms and values into some kind of working relationship with the racist ideology.

In the first instance, the structure of the master-slave society provided the framework for the transformation of Christian norms and values. This transformation took the form of a cleavage of Christian virtues, based on position in society. The strong, virile, and active virtues were assigned to the master, as especially relevant to his structure of living; while the weak and passive virtues were assigned to the slave, as especially relevant to his structure of living. It has already been observed that the portrait of a good Negro which the racist consciousness holds before itself is that of a humble, modest, docile, and deferential person. The racist interpretation of Christian morality, within the structure of the dominance-subservience pattern, has been an important influence upon that portrait. Specifically what a caste society demands in the forms of "Christian characters" is spelled out by Kyle Haselden:

> The white man takes the positive Christian adjectives for himself: noble, manly, wise, strong, courageous; he recommends the passive and negative Christian adjectives to the Negro: patient, long-suffering, humble, self-effacing, considerate, submissive, childlike, meek. It is easy for the white man to think of the Negro as a Christian; but it is difficult, if not impossible, for the white man to think of the Negro in terms of that still choice phrase, a Christian gentleman. This is not to say that the white man does not practice the gentle, the feminine as well as the masculine, Christian virtues; it is to say that he desires in the Negro, not a perfect and complete humanity embracing all the Christian virtues, but a limited humanity which includes only those virtues which will keep the Negro docile and tractable in a subservient role.[40]

[40] Haselden, *The Racial Problem in Christian Perspective* (New York, 1959), pp. 42–43.

The racist consciousness thus selects Christian virtues in terms of their appropriateness for status and role in society. But, since it is the racist ideology which defines racial status and role, the content as well as the form of these virtues is largely influenced by the racist faith. For example, "Christian" nobility in a white man toward a Negro includes social contempt combined with a paternalistic benevolence which rigorously respects the social distance demanded by the caste system. And humility in a Negro means primarily docility and the practice of the expected deference to white people. Only in a quite secondary way does a Negro's humility relate to a general peaceableness in the community. And his humility need not emerge from the spiritual depths of faith and dependence on God at all.

In addition to this corruption of Christian ethics in the form of a double code of morality applying to two distinct groups, three other developments are discussed by Haselden which seriously impair "the white Christian's ability to know what is right and just in his relationship to the Negro." [41]

The first of these is the universal tendency in the Judeo-Christian tradition to limit the demands of the covenantal morality to those specific areas of life in which their practice is reasonably easy. This includes reducing the ethical demand in the most difficult areas of the religious ethic. Much of the prophetic message of the Bible is a call to the people to be faithful to the whole covenant of God, as it relates to all areas of life: there is also the word of judgment upon people for failing to do so. The restriction of the covenantal requirement is a perennial problem of high religion.

The racist faith is related to Christianity in our time in a manner analogous to the relationship between Baalism and the religion of Israel during a large portion of the Old Testament period. Christians have gone "whoring after other gods." Since the Christian racist feels impelled to be loyal to both faiths, he resorts to the perennial urge to isolate Christian morality from some areas of his life, while practicing it in others. In living up to the demands of the racist faith, he must be motivated by pride and contempt, and must engage in social practices which reduce the lives of members of out-races and perpetuate their subordination. In living up to the demands of the Christian faith, he must be motivated by the love of Christ and must engage in social practices which make for the fulfillment of the lives of everyone. Obviously, two contradictory motivations and tendencies cannot be combined in one and the same act of willing and deciding. Therefore

[41] *Ibid.*, p. 49.

it needs only to be said here that in regard to the racial problem as also the other social issues, the white man has restricted the scope of his moral responsibility to members of his own race and reduced the intensity of his ethic to a strictly personal pietism which ignores Christian responsibility for the Negro.[42]

This type of transformation of Christian moral values accounts for the fact that "the extremes of pietism and racial discrimination occupy the same territory." [43]

The second development which impairs the white man's ability to know what is right in race relations has been the dilution of the Christian ethic through the addition of extraneous concepts of gentility. Specifically the notions of propriety and decorum, as prescribed by the racist ethic, have been added to the Christian moral requirement. The tendency to add secular virtues and manners to the religious moral system and to blend them with that system is universal. Medieval feudalism glorified the feudal virtues; in Colonial America, the virtues of the market place were blended and confused with the demands of faith and love. Whenever a social system becomes dominant and pervading, many of the virtues and manners which grow out of that system are blended with the values and demands of the prevailing religious faith. The pervading system of belief and loyalty alongside the Christian faith in America is the racist faith. This faith has described the Negro as an object that is inherently unclean and corrupt. Propriety consequently requires the segregation and quarantine of the Negro.

But the presence of the Negro is desired in a role of subordination. He is wanted as a servant and a menial. There must be some "right way" to relate to him in close contact. Thus the "Christian" moral requirement came to include paternalistic benevolence, on the one hand, and a strict adherence to the social distance taboo in all relationships that savored of equality, on the other. The deep feeling of religious conviction that underlies such behavior is described by Haselden:

Deep in the fibers of his [the Southerner's] soul there is the fear that shaking a Negro's hand, tipping his hat to a Negro woman, sitting at meal with colored people, swimming with them in the same pool, admitting them to his church, may be a mortal sin, "an abuse to the dishonor of God and shame to Christians." [44]

The peculiar feature of this kind of gentility is that it classifies human beings among things to be avoided. Negroes as persons, irre-

[42] *Ibid.*, p. 50. [43] *Ibid.* [44] *Ibid.*, p. 59.

spective of any personal qualities or manifestations of behavior, must be avoided. They are unclean and corrupt from the hand of God. In this distorted form, Christianity contributes to human alienation. It provides neither perspective nor motivation for the reconciliation of man; rather, it lifts his divisions and hostilities to the level of ultimate sanction. A prideful contemptuousness toward some of God's children becomes a Christian virtue.

The third factor which has diluted the moral values of Christian faith in the South is the power of the secular tradition. Haselden affirms that "tradition is reverenced more openly than it is in other areas of the country," and is sacred "in the sense that it has become an integral part of religion." [45] One writer has referred to it in the extravagant terms of "the Shinto Tradition of the American South." Southern tradition is often referred to as "sacred," and when the future is related to it, it is not uncommon to hear the word "eternal" applied.

In a large city in the Deep South, Gunnar Myrdal was a guest at an upper-class luncheon party. At first conversation was free and easy; but eventually someone announced that Myrdal was in America making a study of the race problem. Then, as Myrdal puts it, it became urgent that the situation be redefined. An elderly and very distinguished physician shouldered the responsibility. The discussion became very formal, the doctor's presentation taking the form of a short speech. He denied that there was a "Negro problem" in the South. He asserted that a permanent and static equilibrium had been reached, which corresponded to the inherited abilities and aptitudes of the two races. The relations between the two races, he affirmed, had long since been stratified into "folkways and mores," which the members of both races knew and respected as self-evident and natural.

> The doctor ended up by pointing out that it was, in fact, inherent in the very notion of the "mores," that they could never be questioned or disputed, or even consciously analyzed. There could, indeed, by definition, never be a "problem" concerning the mores of society. The very question was nonsensical. The mores were the ground everybody walked upon, the axioms of social life, even more unquestioned than the religious truths and for more substantial psychological reasons.[46]

In short, it is the word of man that is final in race relations, not the Word of God; and the word of man possesses an impelling power and an intellectual certainty which religious truth cannot share.

[45] *Ibid.*, p. 60.

[46] Gunnar Myrdal, *An American Dilemma* (New York, 1944), p. 33.

E. The racist transformation of democratic values

> The racial question in American society yields to no other problem its place as a primary source of embarrassment both at home and abroad. The contravention by racial discrimination of the values expressed in the American Credo is too obvious for any but the most encysted personalities to ignore.[47]

The contradiction between the racial caste system and the American Creed is the central theme of the *American Dilemma*, the most comprehensive study ever made of the life of the Negro in American society. The author, Gunnar Myrdal, after extensive and intensive research both in the field and in libraries arrived at the conclusion that the "Negro problem" is primarily a moral issue, the distinctive nature of which is an intense conflict of moral valuations.

> The "American Dilemma" referred to in the title of this book, is the ever raging conflict between, on the one hand, the valuations preserved on the general plane which we shall call the "American Creed" where the American thinks, talks, and acts under the influence of high national and Christian precepts, and, on the other hand, the valuations on specific planes of individual and group living, where personal and local interest; economic, social, and sexual jealousies; considerations of community prestige and conformity; group prejudice against particular persons or types of people; and all parts of miscellaneous wants, impulses, and habits dominate his outlook.[48]

That which Myrdal calls the American Creed is not exclusively American; it is American only in the sense that it is adhered to by Americans. Americans do not have a monopoly on the system of ideals embodied in the Creed. With minor variations, the American Creed is the common creed of the democratic West. It is that system of human ideals which is the product of the confluence of the Judeo-Christian tradition and Greek philosophical rationalism, further elaborated by modern philosophical and scientific influences.

Democracy is, of course, a dynamic concept; but it contains certain persistent values, no matter how much the conditions may change to

[47] Kingsley Davis, Harry C. Bredemeier, and Morrison J. Levy, eds. *Modern American Society* (New York, 1949), p. 273. [48] Myrdal, *op. cit.* p. xlvii.

which these values must be applied. Among these values are freedom, equality, justice, and the dignity of the individual, including the idea of self-realization. As a political system, democracy takes the form of government by consent and participation. Since the individual is the unit of society and since rights inhere inalienably in his person, the laws of a democratic state are universally and equally applied.

Americans of every class, race, faith, and region believe in these ideals on, what Myrdal has called, the general and abstract plane of valuation. America must be credited with a high degree of achievement of these values for members of the white race. But in their application to the Negro, these values have been frequently transformed by the conflicting requirements of the caste order.

The first form which the transformation of democratic values takes in relating these values to the Negro is that of the substitution of the mass for the individual. In the racist consciousness no Negro is ever a distinct person; rather, all Negroes are instances of a homogenized mass. Thus all the individualistic conceptions of democracy—rights, property, self-realization, the pursuit of happiness—are applied to Negroes collectively.

The tendency to think of the Negro en masse is so deeply ingrained in American culture that it is practiced by racists and nonracists alike. Obviously the latter do not think and decide on this basis with the same intent and purpose as the former, but they think of and deal with Negroes as a collectivity as certainly as do racists. The racist point of view has so thoroughly permeated institutions and public policy that it has largely smothered the democratic principle of individualism, where the Negro is involved. The present struggle over civil rights in America is an anomaly in the democratic tradition. It is a commentary on the failure of American political democracy to reach the stage of maturity. For democracy is a political system in which the rights of citizens inhere in individuals alone; they do not inhere in groups. When democracy is true to itself, there can be no such thing as "Negro rights" and "the rights of the white man." The rights of citizens do not belong to collectivities; they belong to individuals. Of course, there are collective rights in democratic society, but these are not the rights of citizens as citizens. Rather, they are the rights of institutions and functionaries and are exercisable only in the performance of their special functions and the rendering of their special services. The fact that Negro rights—those same rights which are taken for granted by Caucasian Americans—should now be debated in the highest halls of legislative decision and adjudicated in the highest courts of the land, is history's judgment upon the loyalty of Americans to the principle of individualism, a principle which they otherwise proclaim on the mountaintops and fantically defend.

The development of the individual and his personal contribution to society are persistent ideals of liberal democracy. But the racist consciousness views the development of the Negro as demoralizing to the Negro and a threat to the white man. The self-realization of the Negro is not conceived as helpful to the whole society. Rather, the development of the Negro is thought of as a force which will inevitably pull the white man down. The simple and natural expectations which Negroes have as citizens of America are thus viewed as improper. Through the decades, the segregated society has justified itself on the ground that the Negro is stupid, lazy, and unambitious. But when Negroes in fact manifest intelligence, industriousness, ambition, and drive, the very same people who justify segregated institutions by an appeal to racial stereotypes strike them down.

It is in connection with the idea of the development of the individual that the doctrine of "separate but equal" has been revealed as a gross hypocrisy. Segregated institutions have in truth been separate, but contrary to segregationist claims, they have never been equal. Segregationists have also defended their institutions by saying that they are provided to meet the Negro's peculiar developmental needs. But the fact is, the aim of segregated institutions is to subordinate and thereby deprive just as surely as to isolate. The segregationist regards the Negro as unfit to share the same institutions and functions used and exercised by whites; he also fears the Negro. The segregationist fears that some day he may have to face the awful disclosure of the incorrectness of his judgment. Accordingly, segregated institutions are structured to perpetrate subordination and deprivation. The segregationist feels compelled to deny the resources and agencies of full development to the Negro, lest the Negro really become equal.

In contrast to the denial of individuality in the Negro, the racist consciousness tends to see all relationships of white persons to Negroes as individual and personal from the side of the white person. Racial discrimination—even in its most impersonal, collectivistic, and public forms—is defended under such rubrics as "personal freedom," "the right to choose one's associates," and "the right to private preferences." Nothing confuses the civil rights controversy more than the racist insistence on the extension of the private into the public domain. Civil rights are the rights of persons as citizens. They are impersonal. They belong to all citizens equally and in the same way. The areas in which civil rights are meaningful and applicable are not spheres of personal choice, personal preference, and invitation. On the other hand, all forms of voluntary social relations between persons as persons constitute spheres of invitation, personal preference, common interest, and congeniality. The racist consciousness transforms the civil spheres into areas of social relations, involving personal and private preferences; but it does this only in the context of race relations. The kind of practices involved in this transformation are well summarized by Kyle Haselden:

> . . . We have taken the Negro's "dues" out of the area of his civil rights, where we should be under obligation to honor them, and put them in the area of our social privilege, where we grant them only if we choose to do so. We have refused "to protect a civil right, construing it a social privilege." We use our personal arguments against social leveling to deprive the Negro of his sociological rights. We are opposed to the integration of Negroes and Whites on buses, in trains, and in schools on the basis of personal choice; but this matter lies, not in the area of our social privilege but in the area of the Negro's civil rights. Some people do not want Negroes as close friends or members of the family and construe this personal preference as just cause for excluding Negroes from hotels, restaurants, and churches. They prefer the companionship of members of their own race and conclude that they are therefore justified in barring Negroes from those public and semi-public clubs for which Negroes are disqualified solely on account of their race. They do not want to marry him and conclude that they must therefore deny him the rights of a neighbor.[49]

Racism is organized prejudice and discrimination. It transforms the democratic ideal of freedom to mean the right to deny freedom to others. The racist claims for himself freedom to choose customers, neighbors, schoolmates, and fellow churchmen; but he denies the very same freedom to persons of out-races. The racist is wholly unaware of the private preference, the desire to choose one's associates, the personal aspirations, etc., of persons on the other side of the racial barrier. Beyond the racial boundary no individuals exist to the racist. But even where the racist consciousness is aware of the existence of individuals —within the white race—it denies freedom which contravenes its wishes. The racist will not acknowledge freedom of choice to those white persons who do want to have Negroes as customers, friends, schoolmates, fellow employees, etc. When a society's institutions and

[49] Haselden, *op. cit.*, pp. 59–60.

public life are permeated by the spirit of racism, freedom means obedience to the racist prescriptive system on the part of both the in-race and the out-race. That which racism calls personal freedom is substantially the same as that which communism falls personal freedom. It is independence of decision through submission to collectivist, ideological prescriptions.

In American society—a political community committed to the democratic creed as well as deeply influenced by the racist spirit—it is to be expected that there would be much straining to work out a harmony between the racist and democratic ideals of freedom. To the apparent satisfaction of the racist consciousness, this is achieved by elevating the will of the majority—an instrument of democracy—above the equal and universal application of the laws—democracy's substance. Thus in race relations, a particular policy is adopted as representing "the will of the majority." Since the policy is willed by the majority, it is believed to be democratically valid of itself: inquiry into its substance is considered an impertinence. The fact that the authentic life of democracy is found in its substance, and not in its structures, is forgotten and ignored in the context of race relations. And the fact that the substance of democracy provides guidance for and imposes limitations upon the will of the majority is audaciously rejected.

The final expression of the transformation of the substance of democracy is contained in a statement by Senator George A. Smathers, Democrat of Florida, reported in a newspaper article. Senator Smathers effects this transformation by extending the domain of private prejudice into the area of public policy and by absolutizing the will of the majority. The Senator is quoted as saying that, "he did 'not advocate discrimination against any man.' But he argued that the right to discriminate against Negroes in public accommodations was 'the very heart and lifeblood of liberty' guaranteed by the Constitution." [50] Not only did the Senator from Florida assimilate the Constitution of the United States to racist aims and values in this statement, but he made his statement in "the world's greatest deliberative body," the Senate of the United States. Even a veteran Senator of the United States can become so blinded by the demands and values of the racist faith that he empties the American ideal of liberty of its democratic content when that ideal is applied to Negroes. In the interpretation which the Senator gives to it, liberty comes perilously close to meaning "might makes right." Thus virtually any course of action can be right

[50] E. W. Kenworthy, "The South's Strategy," *New York Times*, March 28, 1964, p. 25.

in a democratic society, if a segment of the citizens has the power and the will to execute it. Thus the American constitutional guaranty of liberty, equality, and equal application of the laws can be eliminated from public policy by racist, aristocratic aims and values.

But the Senator and those who insist that a business man has a right to choose his own customers go beyond the superficial appearance of the might-makes-right doctrine. They go to the full limit of the demands of the racist faith. In effect, those who contend that freedom of enterprise includes the right to choose one's own customers are saying that the Constitution and laws of the United States uphold genocide.[51] It goes without saying that every entrepreneur has the right to be protected as to person and property against the abusive conduct of any and all customers. But no entrepreneur has the right to be protected against the *being* and *presence* of people because he is offended by the form in which God has created them. If the Constitution and laws of the United States uphold this latter right (as many contend they do), in effect the Constitution and laws of the United States uphold genocide because they make possible the total denial of goods and services to people for reasons over which they have absolutely no control. To make genocide a reality, it is only necessary that all the white people of America withhold goods and services from Negroes, beginning at the same time and extending this operation for the same duration. The objection may be raised that this right has seldom been practiced—by grocers, for example—and it is very improbable that it will ever be exercised on a universal scale. But this objection does not meet the fundamental issue. From what faith is the American ideal of liberty to draw its content and substance? If an entrepreneur really does have the unqualified right to choose his customers under the American Constitution, on what principle can the law grant a right to a restaurateur and not to a grocer? Obviously, there is no principle of choice. The grocer has an equal right with the restaurateur to choose his customers. As to the improbability of a racist application of the right to choose one's customers on a universal scale, it must be said that the failure to apply this right universally does not change the fact that the Constitution is being racistically understood, and as long as this is the case, the possibility of the total racist implementation of this right remains.

[51] The phrase "in effect" is used because I am assuming that most persons do not intend genocide, and unhappily most have never thought through the meaning of making freedom of enterprise include the right to choose one's customers according to the nature of their fundamental being.

The major argument of many political leaders in the contemporary American civil rights struggle is their appeal to "States Rights." States rights do in fact constitute a valuable instrument of democracy. The aim of the states rights is to decentralize power and authority and to reflect in public policy the peculiar needs and interests of particular, regional groups of people. In short, state-formed policy is designed to get closer to the substance of democracy. But this instrument which was conceived to make American democracy more effective, has in fact been used historically to deny civil rights to the Negro. Those who defend states rights do so by elevating a political instrument above the very essence which it exists to foster and embody.

F. The sinfulness of racism summarized

Contemporary Christian theology does much speaking of the self-deification of man. But large numbers of Christians have failed to identify self-deification in its purest form, namely, racism. Racism alone claims ultimacy for human being. The deification of the state, a class, or a culture is always the result of some historical construct. Man is continuously building Towers of Babel and, as a consequence, comes "to think of himself more highly than he ought to think" (ROMANS 12:3). But racist man claims ultimacy for the very being which God has given him and refuses to give thanks to God. The fundamental motion of human perversity, says T. F. Torrance, is the ingratitude which presumes that the *imago dei* belongs to man himself, "when it is grounded only in the grace of God." [52] Torrance continues by pointing out that "that was the root of Adam's sin in wanting to make the image of God a matter of his own being." [53] Unthankful arrogance and self-glorification constitute the essential motion of sin. They run "directly contrary to the very motion of the grace of God in which the image of God is rooted and grounded." [54] Racist man makes the daring claim that truth, virtue, and creativity are intrinsic to his being. The good consists in the mere expression of his nature and in keeping his nature pure and uncontaminated. In itself, the being of superior man is sufficient and good. Thus the racist consciousness makes the supreme boast at the very point at which man has done nothing for himself and appropriately can only give thanks.

[52] T. F. Torrance, *Calvin's Doctrine of Man* (new ed.; Grand Rapids, Mich., 1957), p. 114. [53] *Ibid.* [54] *Ibid.*, p. 115.

> . . . Just this is sin; to forget that we are creatures—yes even to misuse the idea of creation by saying that God is in us, that we sense in ourselves divine and creative forces, and by undertaking in the strength of such forces to shape our lives and to build the world. And this sin, this forgetting of his own nothingness, is precisely what really delivers man to nothingness, to death. If he no longer sees God, then all he sees around him is nothing. But he flees from this sight and hides his nothingness from himself. Yet, whoever hides his nothingness always seeks life in the creation instead of from the Creator.[55]

Racism is more than forgetting to give thanks. It is more than the religious indifference which is widespread among men. It is itself religion. It is a decisive act of turning away from God. It is life "according to the flesh" (ROMANS 8:5). It is the worship of "the creature rather than the Creator" (ROMANS 1:25).

> From the standpoint of classical Christian thought, of course, racial prejudice is not one of a catalogue of sins, but is a facet or expression of the single sin of pride, the rejection of the Infinite Sovereign Source of life and the attempt to set up as final some substitute sovereignty derived from the finite. Insofar as fallen, man tends to make of himself or some collective projection of himself the center of love and value. Racial pride within and discriminatory practices are one ready way among many to "exchange the truth of God for a lie," and to worship the creature rather than the Creator.[56]

Racist man presumes upon the prerogatives of God. He rejects the divine sovereignty, and requires that God meet his specifications as to nature and purpose. Racism assumes that man has his life at his own disposal, that he can procure his life by his own power. It is life from the self rather than from God. It is the final expression of fallen man's confidence that he is by himself and for himself. Thus it is the ultimate sin, for the ultimate sin is the rejection of life as the gift of the Creator, based on the false assumption that life is self-procured.

Racism also passes beyond all philosophies of immanence. All notions concerning the presence of the divine Mind or a divine spark in

[55] Rudolf Bultmann, *Existence and Faith*, trans. and ed. Schubert M. Ogden (Cleveland, 1960), p. 180.

[56] Waldo Beach, "A Theological Analysis of Race Relations," in *Faith and Ethics*, Paul Ramsey, ed. (New York, 1957), p. 211.

man assume the presence also of a nondivine or even negative factor. Only racism can conceive of man as pure in the totality of his being. Members of the superior race, who possess an unmixed essence, which is to say, an uncontaminated genetic structure, are unqualified sources of wisdom, virtue, and creativity. There is no taint within them. Pure and superior genes make man wholly pure. His body becomes a glorious body; his mind is the instrument of wisdom, clarity, and creativity.

This attitude of sinful self-reliance issues in a life of continuous boasting. Racists are like the terrible and dreadful Chaldeans: "their justice and dignity proceed from themselves" (HABAKKUK 1:7). They seek to secure their life by standing before God and man in their own strength. They thus are "guilty men, whose own might is their god" (HABAKKUK 1:11). This is, of course, a tragic misjudgment of the human situation. "For who sees anything different in you? What have you that you did not receive? If then you received it, why do you boast as if it were not a gift?" (I CORINTHIANS 4:7.)

Sinful man is in fact under the sway of fear. This is the hidden side of his boasting. He actually cannot find security in his strength and confidence in his greatness. He therefore must whistle loudly in the dark, and stump heavily on the stage of history to prove to himself that he is truly great and strong. In the racist faith the elimination and subordination of out-races is inherently connected with the alleged greatness and glory of the in-race. Racism is inherently a brutal and tyrannical faith. The in-race cannot be its glorious self without the process of extermination and domination of the alleged inferior races. Racist faith issues as inevitably in pessimism and hate as does the Christian faith in hope and love. "The fall of man," says Berdyaev, "finds expression most of all in the fact that he is a tyrant." [57] Only in antithesis does the superior race exist. But since the racist affirmation concerning the polarity of human beings is a false and idolatrous faith and a misconstruction of God's order of creation, only in historical antithesis can the superior race preserve itself. The superior race must be a permanent tyrant.

The sinful tyranny of racism is not only inherent in the racist faith, but where this faith is well domesticated in Christian civilization, it is also blasphemously sanctified by Christianity. In those areas of the world where the pattern of racist domination is old, effective, and where every semblance of revolt has been removed, the sentiments which guide racist domination are baptized by Christianity. This is

[57] Nicolas Berdyaev, *Slavery and Freedom*, trans. R. M. French (New York, 1944), p. 61.

what has happened in the Southern United States, and also to a lesser degree in the rest of the nation. Large numbers of American Christians do not understand the unchristian nature of the racist structure of existence, even in the present hour of ferment and change, because the sentiments and patterns which constitute this structure have been thoroughly baptized. There is a respectable, cultured, and "Christian" form of racial domination, which the harshness of the word "tyranny" does not on the surface seem to fit, because the relationship has been softened by all the sanctions of the culture. The relationship is even thought of as an expression of Christian love; but it actually embodies sentiments which are a tragic perversion of Christian love.

> The respectable, cultured form of racial pride is exactly this paternalistic love, the concern of the superior for the inferior. The Negro neighbor is "loved," is cared for. Thus, in the eyes of the paternalist and churchman the law of Christ is fulfilled in his own behavior. His very kindness is an aid to self-deceit. He is blinded to the corruption at the heart of paternalistic love; that the neighbor is loved, not by reference to God the creator, but by reference to the sinful order of white superiority and Negro inferiority. The neighbor is loved only insofar as he understands the terms of the transaction and "keeps his place." Thus, the mutual love of the order of creation is poisoned at its font by self-love. The resultant paternalism is a disorder of God's basic order of created community.[58]

Thus the racist, who is also a Christian, says in effect to the out-race person, "Meet the criteria which I prescribe and relate to me on precisely the terms which I dictate and I will love you." Accordingly, neither the racist nor his victim are ever able to commune as fellow Christians. Racism is "interposed" between them so that Christian faith cannot find fulfillment. The terms of meeting are not love, but power and submission. The neighbor never comes to be regarded as a member of God's universal community of creation or the Body of Christ. He never becomes a Thou; he is permanently It.

[58] Beach, "A Theological Analysis of Race Relations," in *Faith and Ethics*, p. 213.

CHAPTER VII

Racism and History

A. Race, the foundation of history and civilization

EVER since the publication of Count Arthur de Gobineau's *Inequality of the Human Races* in the 1850's, philosophers have appeared in various Western countries, using race as the key to the interpretation of history. As a naturalistic-humanist faith, racism's exclusive domain of concern is history. When the racist speaks of destiny, he means historic destiny. Racism knows nothing of an ultimate destiny of man, except where it seeks to project its own historic forms and content into eternity by assimilating the Christian hope. In this case, the Christian racist accommodates Christian eschatology to existing racist power arrangements and historic aims.

In the racist philosophy of history, man is not a mere bearer of history under the providence and judgment of the Ultimate, he is history's lord or destroyer. Man appears as a bearer of history only under the guidance of earthly lords. There is no history which is not man's own making or breaking. There is no beginning, center, or end of history wrought by God which gives history its meaning. History must be understood from below. It is the realm of man. "All that is not race in this world is trash. All world historical events, however, are only the expression of the races' instinct of self-preservation in its good or in its evil meaning." [1]

Hitler divides mankind into three groups: culture-founders, culture-bearers, and culture-destroyers. The Aryans alone are hailed as culture-founders, for only Aryans can lay the foundations and provide the es-

[1] Adolf Hitler, *Mein Kampf* (New York, 1940), p. 406.

sential elements of culture. The role of culture-bearers in history is that of adding to the creations of the culture-founders the external forms and colors that reflect the bearers' own characteristics. Culture-bearers can never bring forth the original and essential elements of culture. Even Hitler's wartime friends and "honorary Aryans" must be seen and understood in the proper perspective of the culture-bearers that they are. "It is not the case, as some people claim, that Japan adds European techniques to her culture, but European science and techniques are trimmed with Japanese characteristics." [2] In the strongest possible contrast to the Aryan as the culture-founder stands the Jew as the arch culture-destroyer of history. The Jew has never possessed a culture of his own. The bases for his spiritual and intellectual activity have always been furnished by the culture of others which surrounds him. Drawing upon the thought of Houston Stewart Chamberlain, Hitler sees the Jew as the unique example of the parasite.

In the culture-creating history of the Aryan, even inferior people have an instrumental value. They are not entirely useless. Indeed, they have been valuable auxiliary forces, especially when the Aryan was taking his first steps toward his later culture. Like the service rendered by tamed animals, inferior men did the work which would have been accomplished by technical means, had the technics been available. "Therefore, it is no accident that the first cultures originated in those places where the Aryan, by meeting lower peoples, subdued them and made them subject to his will. They, then, were the first technical instrument in the service of a growing culture." [3] For a lower people, the subjugated state is a genuine improvement, far better than their former so-called freedom.

The view that race is the determinative factor of history is supported by Madison Grant, sometimes referred to as the high priest of American racism. Grant wrote:

> Throughout history, it is only the race of the leaders that has counted and the most vigorous have been in control and will remain in mastery in one form or another until such time as democracy and its illegitimate offspring, socialism, definitely establish cacocracy and the rule of the worst and put an end to progress.[4]

The burden of Grant's thesis is that Europe is in a desperate state of racial affairs and that America must take over Europe's formerly glori-

[2] *Ibid.*, p. 398. [3] *Ibid.*, p. 405.

[4] Madison Grant, *The Passing of the Great Race* (New York, 1921), p. 79.

ous position, since there is still some racial hope left in America. Everywhere in Europe the superior Nordics are receding and being replaced by the inferior Alpines and Mediterranean stocks. Believing that America was founded by Nordics and that the majority of Americans are still Nordic, even at the date of his writing, Grant calls upon America to take over the leadership Europe has lost. But Grant inadvertently discloses the cloven feet of "superior man." He cannot count on the superior race to maintain and expand itself by its own inner quality. He must tie his hope for a natural solution to a political objective—the revision of America's immigration laws. In this objective he succeeded, inasmuch as the influence of the racist ideas of Grant and others became effective in the immigration laws of 1921 and 1924.

The leader of Germany's Third Reich, Adolf Hitler, appears to agree with that part of Grant's thesis having to do with the decay of Germany. The Aryan alone, says Hitler, "was the founder of higher humanity as a whole, thus the prototype of what we understand by the word 'man.' " [5] But unfortunately for Germany, blood poisoning has affected her national body since the Thirty Years' War. This conclusion is in line with the thought of Madison Grant, Lothrop Stoddard, and other American racists who "argued that the 'barbarism' of the Germans during the War [World War I] had been due to the fact that the best elements of the German population have been annihilated during the Thirty Years' War." [6] Hitler deplores the fact that the Old Reich failed to give attention to the true cause of all the really important symptoms of decay. No matter, he says, whether questions of decline and degeneration are economic, cultural, political, or familial; always and everywhere the decay is due to "the non-recognition of racial considerations of one's own people or the non-recognition of a foreign, a racial danger." [7] All efforts at reform and attempts to strengthen the Old Reich failed because the genuine internal health of the nation, that is, its racial health was not taken into account.

The racist philosopher of history both exults in and mourns over the superior race. He rejoices in the conquests, creativity, and civilization-building tendencies of the superior race. But, at the same time, the racist philosopher laments over the impending doom of the master race, which always succumbs at the very moment of success to race mixing and the loss of "racial values." The racist interpretation of his-

[5] Hitler, *Mein Kampf*, pp. 397–398. [6] *Ibid.*, p. 598, footnote of editor.

[7] *Ibid.*, p. 453.

tory is a eulogy to racial greatness, as it looks toward the past, turning into a mournful song as it looks toward the future.

Looking toward the future, as they must, the counter-racist Black Muslims are optimistic. Since they cannot appeal to any past histories of conquest and decay, the Black Muslims are able to indulge in a pure mythology concerning the Black Man as Original Man without recognizing the fact that the "superior race," whether black or white, is doomed by its own self-glorification. The Black Muslims believe that the cessation of wars awaits the world's knowledge of who the Original Man is and the consequential recognition of the rightful owner of the earth.

This is another illustration of the lack of maturity of a mere counter-racism that is out of power. We have already seen that when racism is out of power, it lacks a political plan of action, which is the vital impulse of racism. Weak counter-racism must substitute eschatology for a political plan of action. Now we see that a mere counter-racism lacks the sense of past history and therefore the sense of previous greatness and decay. It therefore is able to indulge in the false hope of a permanent renewal of the race. No historical failures stand between the mythological primitivism of counter-racism and the final restoration of racial greatness.

B. The god of racism is the god of space

> To be means to have space. Every being strives to provide and to preserve space for itself. This means above all a physical location —the body, a piece of soil, a home, a city, a counrty, the world. It also means a social "space"—a vocation, a sphere of influence, a group, a historical period, a place in remembrance and anticipation, a place within a structure of values and meanings. Not to have a space is not to be.[8]

Time and space are inseparable, constituting the main structure of existence, but the most fundamental tension of existence is also sustained between them. The essential quality of time is to have a direction. When time is under the full control of space, it is without direction. The predominance of space over time is mathematically symbolized by the circle. In the life process, this predominance takes the form of the recurring cycle of birth, growth, decay, and death.

[8] Paul Tillich, *Systematic Theology*, Vol. I (Chicago, 1951), p. 194.

The racist philosophy of history is characterized by the cycle of birth, growth, decay, and death. No final resolution of the problem of history within history and no ultimate victory beyond death are conceivable by this philosophy. The master race gives birth to a new culture, it grows to a high degree of greatness; but at this very moment it begins to decay and finally dies because the master race cannot preserve the purity and nobility nature has allegedly endowed it with. There is no power beyond the master race which sustains and renews it, and which might make the final victory of time over space possible. The master race, like inferior races, is totally a product of nature, and possesses its sustaining and creating power exclusively from nature.

What is the meaning of "space" as applied to a political faith?

> Space means more than a piece of soil. It includes everything which has the character of "beside-each-otherness." Examples of spatial concepts are blood and race, clan, tribe, and family. We know how powerful the gods are who give ultimate dignity and value to a special race and to a special community of blood. In all of them the "beside-each-otherness" is dominating.[9]

Racism is a form of paganism, which means "the elevation of a special space to ultimate value and dignity. Paganism has a god who is bound to one place beside and against other places." [10] In the context of race relations, nothing seems to be more urgent to the racist than getting people properly placed. Once this is done, he can proceed to function. He can do business with out-races, help them to improve their lot "in their place," and adjudicate matters between them and members of the in-race. He can even "love" them "in their place."

Every spatial god is imperialistic. The god of one space struggles against what he takes to be the gods of other spaces. Every space is necessarily limited, but an unlimited claim follows because divine honor is given to a particular space. Idols are never universal and sufficient, but they impose the requirement of absolute devotion because they claim absoluteness and universality. Therefore devotion to one requires the exclusion of others. The concept of place in racism does not mean a space on which to stand in order to be. "Place" does not set the boundaries for a community of decision and function. It establishes a system of power and control; in extreme cases, the god of race liquidates other races or removes them from all adjacent spaces. The fully

[9] Paul Tillich, *Theology of Culture*, Robert C. Kimball, ed. (New York, 1959), p. 32. [10] *Ibid.*, p. 31.

expressed will of the god of race is to have the whole earth for himself.

While American racists have never used genocide—the total solution of the space problem—the "back to Africa" and other racial exportation programs have been dear to their hearts. Racists are quick to recognize the disaster entailed when the master race occupies one and the same space with inferior races. No matter how great the social distance that the master race introduces between itself and out-races, the very pattern of dominance and subservience supports dominance and subservience in political, economic, and cultural matters, and in sexual relations as well. While designating Negroes as a valuable element in the community so long as "their place" is one of subservience, Madison Grant nevertheless concludes that "if the purity of two races is to be maintained they cannot continue to live side by side and this is a problem from which there can be no escape." [11] The executive secretary of the Association of Citizens Councils of America says, "Of course the threat of mongrelization won't really be eliminated until the two races are geographically separated." [12] Judge Tom Brady offers specific suggestions for a geographical plan of isolation.

> For instance, [Lower] California could be purchased from Mexico; a territory could be set up in Alaska; islands of the Pacific could be utilized, including the Philippines and Hawaii and there the Negro could be transported. He could be subsidized sufficiently to where he could construct, if possible, a new state.[13]

Retired Rear Admiral John C. Crommelin of Alabama asserts that a back-to-Africa movement would be the best thing for the American Negro, in the absence of which "nothing else would be acceptable but well enforced segregation which I consider a poor substitute." [14] Crommelin also believes that Jews should be exported to Israel or the Malagasy Republic. The editor of *The Thunderbolt* and leader of the National States Rights party predicts that "we will remove all Negroes, Jews, and Orientals from the United States. Then we will open the doors to real immigration from northern Europe to improve our racial stock." [15]

The counter-racist Black Muslims agree with their imperialistic-racist counterparts that races should live in territorial separation. In their thought, however, the evil one is the imperialistic racist. It is he

[11] Grant, *The Passing of the Great Race*, p. 88.

[12] Quoted in James Graham Cook, *The Segregationists* (New York, 1962), p. 50. [13] *Ibid.*, pp. 25–26. [14] *Ibid.*, p. 165. [15] *Ibid.*, p. 178.

who is the scourge of the earth and from whom the nation of Islam must separate before a government of righteousness can be established:

> Separation of the so-called Negroes from their slavemaster's children is a MUST. It is the only SOLUTION to our problem. It was the only solution according to the Bible, for Israel and the Egyptians, and it will prove to be the only solution for America and her slaves, whom she mockingly calls her citizens, without granting her citizenship. We must keep this in our minds at all times that we are actually being mocked.[16]

Elijah Muhammed demands a portion of the United States for the settlement of Negroes and the establishment of a Black Republic. A few states are requested to provide the territory and material assistance for a period of twenty or twenty-five years until the new state and civilization can be firmly established. Muhammed believes that this is not at all too much to ask as compensation for the four hundred years of exploitation which has been perpetrated upon the Negro.

The idea that races must have their own spaces is universal in the racist circle of faith; but Madison Grant goes beyond this notion to affirm that by Nature each race does have a space. "The laws which govern the distribution of the various races of man and their evolution through selection are substantially the same as those controlling the evolution and distribution of the larger mammals." [17] Races have natural habitats in which they achieve their highest development. The habitat of the Nordic, "the superior race," is in the North where there is a large amount of moisture, snow, and a constant variety of temperature. Grant concedes that the Nordic can live outside his natural environment, but when the Nordic does, he must be in the position of a land-owning aristocrat. As history's natural aristocrat, and therefore the man who is needed everywhere, the proper space of the Nordic outside his natural habitat is *above*. When the Nordic lives in the same space with inferior races, his appropriate space is *above* and theirs is *below*.

But, as we have seen, this is not the happiest solution of the space problem.

> Where two distinct species are located side by side history and biology teach that but one of two things can happen; either one race drives the other out, as the Americans exterminated the In-

[16] *The Supreme Wisdom,* II, 39. Quoted in Essien-Udom, *Black Nationalism* (Chicago, 1962), p. 259. [17] Grant, *The Passing of the Great Race,* p. 37.

dians and as the Negroes are now replacing the whites in various parts of the South; or else they amalgamate and form a population of race bastards in which the lower type ultimately preponderates.[18]

When the god of space truly reigns over his own, he makes an unqualified and absolute claim to his space. Only the absolute claim is adequate.

> Australia and New Zealand, where the natives have been virtually exterminated by the whites are developing into communities of pure Nordic blood and will for that reason play a large part in the future history of the Pacific. The bitter opposition of the Australians and Californians to the admission of Chinese coolies and Japanese farmers is due primarily to a blind but absolutely justified determination to keep those lands as white man's countries.[19]

In contrast to the deification of the space of the in-race, the space of the out-race is demonized. Any space occupied by members of out-races is bad by nature, simply because they occupy it. Accordingly, every Negro neighborhood is a blighted area. It does not matter what the character and personal commitments of the inhabitants are, their neighborhood is blighted because they are there. Every job, traditionally held by members of out-races, is bad for that very reason. Purity of being spells purity of space, defectiveness of being spells defectiveness of space.

C. Meaningful history in Christian faith

The racist search for meaning is man's supreme effort to find his security and fulfillment in himself. Truth, value, and meaning are man's own creations. He and he alone is their sole source. History is meaningful insofar as the products, processes, structures, ideals, values, and ideas of civilization are the direct expression of the hereditary strains of the superior race. Inferior races are related to the creativity and culture-building of the superior race, but only as useful and obedient instruments. Intermediate groups may serve a higher function, but theirs is at best a culture-bearing role.

The Christian understanding of history is diametrically opposed to

[18] *Ibid.*, p. 77. Grant does not indicate why the "lower type" should ultimately preponderate. [19] *Ibid.*, p. 79.

this view. Christian faith knows nothing of autonomous man. On the contrary, Christian faith affirms that man is a dependent creature who is alienated from his Creator. The very act of declaring his self-sufficiency, as in racism, is the essence of his alienation; for in this act he violates the truth of his existence, which is to be for God.

According to Christian faith, history is meaningful when and where men respond to the sovereign action of God. The sovereignty of God is expressed in a series of mighty acts. The God of the Christian faith is the God who called Abraham from Ur of the Chaldeans. He delivered the children of Israel from Egypt. He made a covenant with them. From time to time he sent his prophets to call them to repentance. And at last, "when the times were fulfilled," He sent His Son into the world to redeem the world. It is this last of God's mighty acts which constitutes the supreme revelation of the meaning of existence. Through the life, death, and resurrection of Christ, the meaning of man's historic existence is disclosed and fulfilled.

In contrast to racist faith, Christianity asserts that the meaning of history is not completed within history. On the one hand, meaning must come into history from beyond history; on the other, meaning is never fulfilled within history, for history's goal lies beyond itself.

> In Christian faith the place of Christ as both the revelation of the character of God and of the essential nature of man (the "second Adam") does justice to the fact that man can find his true norm only in the character of God but is nevertheless a creature who cannot and must not aspire to be God. The God who is his norm is God as He is revealed in a character of human history, that is, in Christ. Christ is at once an historical character and more than an historical character. His life transcends the possibilities of history but it remains relevant to all historical striving, for all historical goals can be expressed only in supra-historical terms. If stated in purely historical terms they will embody some contingency of nature and history and set a false limit for the human spirit.[20]

Christ is thus the Lord of history. Those who respond to Him in the obedience of faith become bearers of meaning. They are never the source and fulfillment of meaning; they are bearers of meaning as they live in faith, hope, and love in the union of His Body. History has meaning wherever and whenever men can say in faith, "To live is Christ" (PHILIPPIANS 1:21). But the Christian can recognize that Christ

[20] Reinhold Niebuhr, *The Nature and Destiny of Man,* Vol. I (New York, 1944), pp. 163–164.

is his life only in the experience of the tension between the Yes and the No. "It is the 'yes' of creation, atonement and redemption, and the 'no' of the condemnation and death of the life which has fallen away from its origin, its essence and its goal." [21] True meaning and reality belong to Christ alone. He alone incarnates the meaning of existence. The true life of the Christian is not his own; it is outside himself; it is in Jesus Christ. The Christian man receives it and continues by grace to receive it as bestowed life.

On the other hand, the self-appointed lordship of racist man must be viewed as utter blasphemy. Prophetic faith proclaims the divine judgment above all upon those who blaspheme God by taking His place as the lords of the earth.

> Judgment in history falls heaviest on those who come to think themselves gods, who fly in the face of Providence and history, who put their trust in manmade systems and worship the work of their own hands, and who say that the strength of their own right arm gave them the victory. We are speaking of an interim judgment taking place within the historical sphere and I am not saying it is a final assessment; but supposing there is a man like Hitler and we can concede that he may be utterly unselfish in his passion for his country, still, if there is a moral judgment in history it tells us repeatedly that such a man by aping providence blasphemes God, and brings more rapid tragedy on the world and on himself, than the people who give half their lives to wine, women, and song.[22]

Christian faith recognizes that the executions of moral judgments in history are inexact. Good and innocent people do suffer along with the bad. Unoffending nations are overrun by superior power. Yet faith perceives that the divine sovereignty as judgment is not pure mystery, "since the experiences of life, in which egotism and self worship are punished, are in rough and inexact relation to the ultimate judgment upon the self, perceived by the self in the experience of repentance and faith." [23]

Through the eyes of faith, man learns that it is man who thwarts himself. It is man's refusal to accept his finitude and dependence which is his primal sin. That which may be called the "necessity of history"

[21] Dietrich Bonhoeffer, *Ethics*, Eberhard Bethge, ed. (New York, 1955), p. 190.

[22] Herbert Butterfield, *Christianity and History* (New York, 1950), p. 60.

[23] Reinhold Niebuhr, *Faith and History* (New York, 1949), p. 132.

or history's fateful element grows in part out of man's own self-will; and probably may be traced wholly to self-will, if all the conflicts and ambiguities of history could be taken into account. At any rate, Christian faith knows, in contrast to the lordly confidence of racism, that the "necessities of history" prevent man from being the lord of history that racist man claims to be and would like to be. The more man strives and the more certain he seems to be able to take history into his own hands, the more disastrous will be his defeat.

> It is a strange irony of our time that all progress in science and civilization, nay, in moral and social consciousness, is turned eventually into a means for war and destruction. Even those peoples who do their utmost to prevent such tragic reversal are forced to submit to the necessity of history. To the extent to which man, through his reason, has learned to control nature, he has fallen victim to the catastrophes of history. Thus his dream that he may be entirely free to shape his future according to the ideals of his own reason is frustrated by history. Man is thwarted by himself, by his own nature.[24]

In contrast to the racist god of space, the God of Christian faith is the God of time. Only the God of time can be truly sovereign and the source of universal meaning and purpose. The god of space must in the nature of the case exist alongside other gods of space, even if he is the most powerful among them. He is in reality only a projection of racial, tribal, or national interest and purpose. He is inseparable from the people of whom he is the projection. He has no hands, no feet, no mind, no purpose save theirs. The god of space is doomed to disaster and defeat because he is a constellation of false meaning and purpose. Man can never secure and fulfill himself in any space because man is not fundamentally a child of space. Man is created for fellowship with God. His true home and destiny are beyond space. Every effort on his part to secure and fulfill himself in space is a violation and repudiation of his destiny as man.

The Christian God of time is the transcendent ground and end of the universe. He is the maker of the heavens and the earth; He sends the seasons; He determines times and places. The action of the God of time is sovereign because it is directed toward the goal which He himself has set. The identification of the God of time with a particular space or people and their interests is a denial of the divine sovereignty

[24] Erich Frank, *Philosophical Understanding and Religious Truth* (New York, 1945), p. 121.

and a rejection of the divine purpose. The command to Abraham to leave his homeland is

> the command to leave the gods of soil and blood, of family, tribe and nation; that is, the gods of space, the gods of paganism and polytheism, the gods who stand beside each other—even if one of them is the most powerful. The true God who spoke to Abraham cannot be identified with a family or city-god. In the moment in which the danger of such an identification arises, God must separate Himself from those who adore Him. The representative of this separation is the prophet. He does not deny the God of his fathers, but he protests against the abuse of this God by the priests of soil and blood, of tribe and nation. He pronounces the separation of God from His nation. This becomes obvious in the great prophets who announce the complete rejection of the nation by God if it continues as a pagan cult with pagan ethics and politics.[25]

The monotheism of the prophets is the monotheism of justice. The gods of space are inevitably unjust because, while each is limited and the guardian of a particular people, nevertheless each makes unlimited and expansionist claims and thus destroys the universalism of justice.

> The prophetic threat against the elected nation, that it will be rejected by God because of injustice, is the real victory over the gods of space. . . . Tragedy and injustice belong to the gods of space; historic fulfillment and justice belong to the God who acts in time and through time, uniting the separated space of his universe in love.[26]

Since biblical faith understands history as the sphere of decision, and since it understands the individual as a part of humanity as a whole, the essential historical elements are decision and community. The context of person is community; it is not Nature or the world, or the Idea. And since God is the origin and destiny of the human person, historical decision is profoundly serious. Every decision is momentous, for it is an act of responsible obedience or an act of rebellion.

The faith by which the individual perceives his responsibility before God is the faith by which he perceives his solidarity with mankind. Pride is impossible in the life of faith because those of the Christian community of faith know that they are all Adam and the past is the guilt which they all bear. To the eyes of faith, mankind is not di-

[25] Tillich, *Theology of Culture*, pp. 35–36. [26] *Ibid.*, p. 38.

vided into groups of the corrupt, on the one hand, and the pure, on the other. ". . . all have sinned and fall short of the glory of God" (ROMANS 3:23), and all share in a solidarity of guilt. But guilt and condemnation are not the last words of God. Through Christ there is a solidarity of redemption as well as guilt. We are one in Adam, but through the gift of grace we become one in Christ. Whenever and wherever this happens, a new depth of meaning appears in history. Life is found, and it awaits the final consummation.

CHAPTER VIII

The Renewal of Man

A. The racist approach to the renewal of man

In the racist philosophy, the fall means "racial impoverishment." The fall consists in "blood poisoning," the mixing of the blood of the superior race with that of inferior races. Accordingly, the essence of redemption is racial renewal, the revivification of the superior race by techniques of purification.

In the language of Lothrop Stoddard, the renewal of man calls for the development of the "Neo-Aristocracy." In the past, he affirms, harsh measures, such as the summary execution of criminals, the lack of proper care and medical attention for the weakly child, and the violent treatment of the insane, "kept the germ-plasm of the race reasonably purified." [1] Today, Stoddard continues, the physical, mental, and moral cripples of the race are preserved at public expense. In the earlier days the bloody hand of natural selection would have wiped out these wastrels. But in the present situation which preserves "wastrels," "factors like birth control, education, and high social standards are simultaneously extirpating the superior elements at an unprecedented rate." [2]

In answering the question posed by himself, "What now is to be done?" Stoddard proposes a program of eugenics. The champion of the new era is the science of biology. From thousands of laboratories and library alcoves "have emerged discoveries which may completely

[1] Lothrop Stoddard, *The Revolt against Civilization* (New York, 1922), p. 91.
[2] *Ibid.*, p. 92.

alter human destiny."[3] Stoddard speaks of these discoveries in the exalted terms of "the new biological revelation" and says in effect that they disclose the meaning of human existence. "Here indeed, is something new: the unveiling of the mysteries of the life process, the placing in man's hands of the possibility of his own perfection by methods at once safe and secure."[4]

In the broad field of cultural institutions and ideas, the eugenic program calls for a revaluation of values. Legal, social, and economic adjustments must be made. The program consists in two distinct parts, designated as "positive" and "negative" eugenics. "Positive" eugenics is the process of race building or the multiplication of superiors. "Negative" eugenics is the process of race cleansing or the elimination of inferiors.

Although race building is the trancendent interest in "race betterment," race cleansing is the starting point demanded by the realities of the situation. "Here scientific knowledge is most advanced, the need for action most apparent, and public opinion best informed."[5] The first step in race cleansing should be the prevention of child bearing on the part of all obvious degenerates. If this is to be effective, they must be segregated in institutions. A beginning has already been made in the segregation of the insane and feeble-minded in public institutions. But the campaign against degeneracy must be greatly extended to include physical and mental unsoundness.

The second step in "negative" eugenics is to debar the less obvious defectives from having children. The less obvious defectives constitute the vast "outer fringe" of unsoundness. Stoddard does not believe that public opinion is ready to take this second step, but is hopeful that once it sees the good results of the first step, further advances along the same line will be possible. In the long run, legal measures to remove the higher grades of unsoundness will not be necessary. "The very conversion of public opinion to the eugenic viewpoint would itself tend powerfully to purify the race by voluntary action."[6] In a society in which the true racial consciousness is developed in the general population

> the begetting of unsound children would be regarded with horror, and public opinion would instinctively set up strong social taboos which would effectively restrain all except reckless and anti-social individuals—who, of course, would be restrained by law.[7]

[3] *Ibid.*, p. 238. [4] *Ibid.* [5] *Ibid.*, p. 245. [6] *Ibid.*, p. 250.
[7] *Ibid.*, p. 251.

The enactment of a program of race building or perfecting is more difficult than race cleansing. Stoddard admits this. Even the theoretical formulation of such a program is difficult. The difficulty is reflected in Stoddard's inability to be as specific concerning the content of race building as he is concerning race cleansing. Only one line of action is suggested for society as a whole—the remission of taxation to families proportionate to the production of "desirable" children. This should be done with great care, however. "Only where the racial superiority of the couples in question is clearly apparent as shown by proven ability, psychological tests, and sound heredity, should such subsidies be granted." [8] In no case should large families be subsidized, regardless of their racial value.

In addition to this legal course of action, society must rely on the "eugenic conscience" itself for race building and perfecting. "The great thing is to get people to thinking racially. With the development of a 'eugenic conscience' and the curbing of degeneracy, plans for race building will almost formulate themselves." [9]

The eugenic ideal is an "ever-perfecting super race," not a static reality. Upon the foundation of this new genetic substructure, an undreamed of cultural superstructure will be erected. "Every phase of human existence will be transformed: laws and customs, arts and sciences, ideas and ideals, even man's conception of the Infinite." [10]

As a part of the plan to establish America as the heir to the greatness and glory once enjoyed by Europe, Madison Grant also calls for the introduction of the ideal and practice of eugenics.[11] The value and efficiency of a population, he says, are not assessed by the number of souls, as the newspapers suppose, "but by the proportion of men of physical and intellectual vigor. The small Colonial population of America was, on an average and man for man, far superior to the present inhabitants, although the latter are twenty-five times more numerous." [12] Statesmanship must accordingly direct itself toward the improvement of quality, not quantity.

Grant rejects the idea that human life has either the intrinsic value proclaimed by philosophical idealism or the derivative value proclaimed by biblical faith. "The laws of nature require the obliteration

[8] *Ibid.*, p. 256. [9] *Ibid.* [10] *Ibid.*, p. 263.

[11] The other part of the plan—the reorganization of immigration laws so that they favor northern Europeans—has already been referred to.

[12] Grant, *The Passing of the Great Race* (New York, 1921), p. 48.

of the unfit and human life is valuable only when it is of use to the community or race." [13] The failure to eliminate defective infants and to sterilize adults who are of no value to the community has been due to "mistaken regard for what are believed to be divine laws and a sentimental belief in the sanctity of human life." [14] Altruism, philanthropy, and the influence of the Church have been the factors behind an indiscriminate charity for the benefit of the individual. Grant asserts that this line of thinking could be defended before eugenics were understood. But now that the science of eugenics is available, the societies for charity and the extension of rights must have some small modicum of brains in their management or they will continue to do "more injury to the race than black death or smallpox." [15]

By means of a rigid system of selection, the whole question of the unfit could be solved in a century. The state should sterilize all social discards, "beginning always with the criminal, the diseased and the insane and extending gradually to types which may be called weaklings rather than defectives and perhaps ultimately to worthless racial types." [16]

Two methods of race improvement are open to man. "He can breed from the best or he can eliminate the worst by segregation or sterilization." [17] Grant concludes that the method of race improvement open to man under existing conditions is the elimination of the least desirable elements of society through deprivation of their power of procreation.

In the counter-racist faith of the Black Muslims, the hope for the renewal of man inverts the hope of aggressive white racism and reflects the present sociopolitical position of the former. As a people who are the victims of oppression, deprivation, and manipulation, the beginning of renewal for the Black Muslim is the transformation of the present generation. In its first stage, renewal takes the form of the achievement of self-identity. The most pronounced characteristic of Black Muslims "is a desire for a personal rebirth—an escape to a new identity, in which they will be freed of their present restrictions and oppressions." [18] Since American society has tended to homogenize the personalities of the Negro masses, the hope that selfhood may be gained through individuality has probably never entered the consciousness of the majority of the most dispossessed. The Black Muslim

[13] *Ibid.*, p. 49. [14] *Ibid.* [15] *Ibid.*, p. 50. [16] *Ibid.*, p. 51.

[17] *Ibid.*, pp. 51–52.

[18] C. Eric Lincoln, *Black Muslims in America* (Boston, 1961), p. 100.

accordingly gains his new self "by adopting a powerful corporate identity." [19] One and the same thing "is indispensable to a creative life for the individual and for the group, and is the true meaning of heaven." [20] That one thing is the knowledge of one's own identity, which is the knowledge of the self, nation, religion, and God.

The second stage in the Black Muslim plan of renewal points toward the future fulfillment. The Black Muslims are realistic enough not to claim racial purity at the present time. But the repurification of the "Lost Nation in the West" is the great promise of the future. At present they are greatly exercised about the degree to which the white man has already mixed his blood with that of the black man. The strategy to meet this situation is separation. The present plight of the black masses demands that they separate from the white man by stages, but there must be an immediate end to all personal relationships between the races. Convinced of their "superior racial heritage," the Black Muslims

> believe that a further admixture of white blood will only weaken the Black Nation physically and morally, as well as increase the loss of face the so-called Negro has already suffered by permitting the white man to bastardize the race. The white race will soon perish, and then even a trace of white blood will automatically consign its possessor to an inferior status.[21]

As soon as they receive the teachings of Elijah Muhammed, Black Muslims "begin to enjoy the Resurrection and the Hereafter." [22] The resurrection means the moral, spiritual, and material transformation which the Black Muslim community effects in the lives of its constituents. The Hereafter, however, is present only in imagination for it will be the period after the destruction of the present world. It is the consummation toward which Black Muslims bend their present preparations. It is life "under a ruler and government of righteousness after the destruction of the unrighteous." [23]

[19] *Ibid.*, p. 101.

[20] Essien-Udom, *Black Nationalism* (Chicago, 1962), p. 123.

[21] Lincoln, *op. cit.*, p. 89.

[22] Essien-Udom, *Black Nationalism*, pp. 137–138.

[23] *Ibid.*, p. 137.

B. Divine judgment in the racist life

The wrath of God is the strange work of His love. The judgment of God is therefore fully known only to faith. Only the man of faith can know in the depths of his being what it means to fall. Only he who abides in the divine love can perceive the full meaning of rebellion and alienation. But this does not mean that God confronts only the faithful as judge. It does not mean that God has a claim only on the faithful. God confronts all men as judge because He lays claim on all men as their Creator and because all men have rebelled against Him. Furthermore, all men know, albeit dimly, that God claims them. Accordingly the uneasy conscience and the striving for self-justification are universal and perennial.

When, however, the worship of idols emerges in the covenant community, the Lord God appears mightily in the midst as troubler and accuser. In the constellation of racist meanings and values, justification by grace through faith is turned into the desperation of self-justification in racial pride.

The effort of racist man to justify himself before man has already been observed in the discussion of the justifications of segregation. But self-justification in the sight of man is never sufficient for man. This is especially true if the self-justifying consciousness is also a religious consciousness devoted in some areas of its life to the Christian faith. Such a person feels that he must do more than justify his racism before men, he must also justify it before God. Often this need "takes the form of the pietism of the Christian churchman, who will attempt to overcome the opposition between Christian morality and racial prejudice by a preoccupation with transcendent moral principles, avoiding all local application." [24] The watchword of this approach to Christian morality is, "if men would only give their hearts to the Lord Jesus, all of these social problems would be solved." [25] In fact, the exponents of such pious sentiments have indulged in a spiritual self-deception of such proportions that they cannot see that there are any problems to solve. Segregation and the whole order of racial caste practices have become amoral in their perspective. Race relations and sometimes other social problems "have nothing to do with religion." They are merely "natural forms of human adjustment" or "our way of doing things." [26] Such

[24] Waldo Beach, "A Theological Analysis of Race Relations," in *Faith and Ethics*, Paul Ramsey, ed. (New York, 1957), p. 217. [25] *Ibid.* [26] *Ibid.*

judgments are possible because the covenantal faith of Christianity has been restricted to a religion of inwardness and an aesthetic appreciation of transcendent principles. There are requirements in the outer life; but these are largely confined to the family, the primary relationships of neighborhood and club, and "churchmanship."

Thus the self-justification, which the polytheism of Christianity and racism makes urgent, pierces the Christian faith of the devotee at its heart. The Christian doctrine of justification by grace through faith is diametrically opposed to all forms of self-justification as to source, motive, power, and direction. The grace which justifies is the free gift of God. It is a gift which must be received by the total person in the act of surrender, but it never becomes a possession. To have faith and to be empowered by grace mean to be possessed rather than to be a possessor. Justification by grace through faith involves a having and a not having. We have the grace of God only insofar as we are continuously receiving it. The Christian is one who hungers and thirsts after righteousness, and he is continuously being filled (cf. MATTHEW 5:6). This righteousness is forever outside himself. It is the righteousness of Christ. His justification means that the righteousness of Christ is imputed to him. As a justified sinner, he knows that he must continuously "hold fast" to Christ and be renewed. On the contrary, the self-justification which racism induces, and which is frequently domesticated within Christianity, is a form of self-elevation based on piety as a self-possession. Justification as God's own gracious act is denied. The religious consciousness claims a possession over *against* God, even if it believes that the possession originally came *from* Him.

The judgment of God is also discernible to the eyes of faith in the fact that the Churches have long since been "cast out and trodden under the foot of man" in the field of race relations.[27]

> It is a dogma taken for granted by most sociologists that religion is a function of culture. And in fact this is confirmed by the actual behavior of the churches which the sociologist encounters, for what he discovers is the "escapism" of Negro churches, with their practices compensatory for cultural frustrations, and the inertia of the white churches.[28]

Happily the Churches have recently begun to manifest a new moral vitality in race relations, but their historical record in this field has predominantly been characterized by cultural accommodation. Theolo-

[27] Beach, "A Theological Analysis of Race Relations," in *Faith and Ethics*, p. 218. [28] *Ibid.*

gians, historians, and Churchmen have attested to this fact as have sociologists.

The latter half of the nineteenth century was a period of great moral reform in the United States. Many abolition societies were included among the reform movements. Frequently, these groups and others found a resistance to their efforts within the Churches that was so stubborn they were forced to withdraw and ally themselves with movements outside the Churches, or to reconstitute themselves along secular lines. In this mid-twentieth-century revolution in race relations, the initial vitality has come from secular agencies. The earlier achievements of desegregation of the last two decades were prompted and implemented by and embodied in legal, judicial, economic, and educational institutions. Many Churches have recently entered the field as active partners of movements of moral reform in race relations. But large numbers of Churches still admonish their members to obey desegregation edicts simply because "they are the law of the land." Through eyes that have been blinded by the domestication and assimilation of racism within their own faith and life, these Churches fail to see that racism is a profoundly spiritual tragedy. They cannot understand that racism is the prototype of human alienation and that segregation is the principal structural expression of alienation. Due to their own perversity in race relations, the light that is in them has become darkness (cf. MATTHEW 6:22). Such Churches give substance and validity to the claim that religion is only a function of culture.

Divine judgment in race relations may also be seen in the social response which racial injustice evokes. Faith-seeking knowledge understands that history does not yield exact moral balances. Kindness is not always met with kindness; virtue is not always rewarded; honesty frequently does not "pay." Furthermore, even when a genuine effort is made to vindicate justice, such a judgment is inexact because of the sinful blindness of man and because there is no earthly organ of justice in which righteousness and power inhere in perfect balance. But insofar as those who are oppressed aim at genuine justice in their efforts to remove their oppression, their action is a fragmentary vindication of divine judgment. Thus

> God judges white pride through the Negro's response to that pride. Just as in international life the Christian sees God's hand in the power of Communism as a judgment on the sins of capitalist democracy, or colonial imperialism, so in modern racial life the Christian of sensitive and contrite Spirit can acknowledge the divine chastisement upon his own sin and that of his people in the recent

rise of aggressive Negro leadership, demanding equal rights and equal status.[29]

While only the eyes of faith can see the meaning of human decision and action in relation to the divine sovereignty and purpose, nevertheless the natural light of reason can discern the personal, social, political, and economic losses which result from the racist system of loyalty and practice. The fact that the racist structure of relationships is a contradiction of the divine will for community is seen in a faint shadow within the limits of the social and psychological sciences under the rubric of personal and sociocultural losses. Among these are the loss of rational integrity through prejudice; the false self-image which racist pride engenders and the consequential pretenses to a wisdom, virtue, and security which do not in fact exist; the truncation of the individuality of the self as well as the other; and the false diagnosis of personal and social problems and the consequential erroneous application of solutions. Of course, the racist believes that he is gaining something by means of his prejudice and discrimination. But alleged gains are rooted in structures of human relationship that are morally and spiritually degenerate, and that reduce the life of both the victim and the perpetrator of evil.

In addition to these untoward results in the life of the individual, racism imposes great losses upon society as a whole. The economic cost of maintaining a system of prejudice and discrimination is incalculable. A society which arbitrarily deprives a sector of its population denies itself increased productivity and economic well-being. A society which withholds opportunity for development from any of its potential scientists, artists, administrators, theologians, and philosophers makes itself the poorer. No one can ever know how much closer we would now be to a cure for cancer if, for just two generations, America had fully employed the scientific imagination and creativity of its Negro population. It has been said that "the mills of the gods grind slowly, but exceedingly fine." The whole world today faces an ominous future. There is the awful possibility of world destruction through nuclear war. Whether this possibility shall come to pass is wholly a spiritual question, though the means are technological. And the question is the same whether the world survives or is destroyed. If man continues to choose the way of pride, self-deification, and falsehood, there will be the judgment of destruction and tyranny. Of central importance in this unhappy possibility is whether man continues to worship at the shrine of racism.

[29] *Ibid.*, p. 217.

C. The Body of Christ in racist society

The Church is the dominion of Christ on earth. It is His continuing work through the ages. Christ and His Church belong together; the existence of the Church is in and through Him. The Church is where Christ is; and where Christ is, there is the Church.

To express the idea of the inseparable unity of Christ and His Church, the Christian community has employed from New Testament times the symbol of the "Body of Christ." In Ephesians and Colossians, Christ is referred to as the "head of the body, the church." This phrase is not intended, as is sometimes supposed, to separate or to distinguish Christ from His Church. Rather, it means that Christ and His Church are in indissoluble unity. It does not mean that a part of the life of the Church is allocated to Christ and another part to the Church. The Church is not a body with a foreign and exchangeable head. It is the Body of Christ. It therefore can have no other head but Christ, for the Body of Christ is Christ himself.

The Christian fellowship is then the true Church when it serves Christ, when it is obedient to its head. The Church is never the Rev. John Doe's church on Juniper Street. No Church of Christ belongs to any man, group, race, class, or ecclesiastical order. The Church of the Living God is the Body of Christ. He and He alone is its head. To be called of Christ and united with His Body, the Church, is to have no other authority but Christ.

The Holy Spirit is the power who creates the Church and renews it. Where the Spirit is at work, there is the Church. Christ is alive and at work in His Church where the members know the power of the Spirit in their lives. If there is anything in the historic Church which does not bear the stamp of the Spirit, it is condemned by faith. On the day of Pentecost, the disciples became a new people by the power of the Holy Spirit. The Spirit created the Church, brought forth the fruits of the Spirit, and continues to create and renew the Church through the ages. The Church is never built or preserved by men.

As the community which continues the work of Christ on earth, the Church is also catholic, or universal. Both the finished work of Christ on the cross and His continuing work in His Church are universal. "God was in Christ reconciling the world to himself" (II CORINTHIANS 5:19). Christ sent His disciples into all the world to make disciples of all nations. And the community of love which is called into being by His Spirit knows no boundaries nor barriers. "Here there cannot be Greek and Jew, circumcised and uncircumcised, barbarian, Scythian, slave, free man, but Christ is all, and in all" (COLOSSIANS 3:11). The victory of the divine love in Christ is universal in scope. When Christian faith is real it can draw no boundaries around the Church. Since God was in Christ reconciling the world unto Himself, there are no boundaries. Even death is not a boundary. We are surrounded by a cloud of witnesses (cf. HEBREW 12:1). The fellowship includes the witnesses to the faith in all ages and in all places. The activity of the Holy Spirit through the gospel fixes the boundaries of the Church. And this is to say that there are no boundaries, for the redemptive love of God extends to all.

The Church cannot be understood in terms of the qualities and activities of the individuals who make up its membership. When men set up human qualifications as requisite for the formation and growth of the Church, they are seeking to build the Body of Christ on their own terms. They are seeking to construct from below that which can come only from above. They are rejecting the Holy Spirit of Christ which faith knows to be the only creative and constitutive factor of the Church. Furthermore, when men arrogate the right to decide upon their own criteria for Church membership, they thereby transfer the authority of the Holy Spirit to the authority of men and they substitute the word and spirit of men for the Word and Spirit of God. This is precisely what is done when men decide that the criteria for the formation and growth of the Church shall be race, class, nationality, or social congeniality. The authority over the Church is thus taken from Christ and placed in the hands of men. Men become the heads of the Body and substitute their call and election for the call and election of God. They seek to build and maintain from below that which can only exist as the gift of God.

Protestant Churches in America sometimes indulge in a form of self deception by which they hide their racially exclusivistic membership policies from themselves by affirming the exclusivism of class. This process is aptly described by Kyle Haselden:

> In our day there is a strange and disturbing development, particularly among Protestant Christians. The rare Negro who is accepted as an equal in the white Protestant church must first qualify socially or professionally. He escapes the stigma of race only by achieving the standard of class; or, so to speak, he ceases to be the excluded "Jew" only by becoming the acceptable "Greek."

> It is required of the Negro applicant, not that he prove himself as a Christian, but primarily that he match in his life the cultural stratum which characterizes the particular church to which he applies. Thus the socially stratified Protestant church violates that catholicity which the Apostle required, even in the seemingly tolerant act of accepting a Negro into its membership.[30]

The self-deception in this process lies in the fact that it sustains both racial and class discrimination, while those who indulge in it delude themselves into believing that they have done something noble and virtuous. The class discrimination is obvious, but racial discrimination also continues in two forms. First, such a Church-membership policy is usually a form of "tokenism." There is no disposition to accept more than a very small number of Negroes, even from among those who qualify as "Greeks." Second, a Negro applicant's cultural credentials are more rigorously scrutinized than those of white applicants, and middle-class characteristics are more rigorously demanded of him. In perhaps the majority of such cases, working-class white persons are in the membership.

When it is said that no human qualifications can earn membership in the Body of Christ, this must be understood to include even religious qualities. The saints are those who belong to God, not those who have achieved freedom from sin. They are justified, yet sinners. They are those who by the grace of God have been incorporated into the new life of the covenant community. The saints belong to God because they have been called and elected by Him. "You did not choose me, but I chose you" (JOHN 15:16). The saints are wholly without qualifications of their own creation. The holiness of the saints is not their own. Christ alone is the Holy One of God. The holiness of the Church depends on the Holy Spirit who is active in the Church. It derives from the fact that the Lord himself is present and realizes the work of redemption in His Church. On that occasion when the disciples of Jesus came to Him, saying, "Who is the greatest in the kingdom of heaven?" (MATTHEW 18:1), the Master replied, saying, "Truly, I say to you, unless you turn and become like children, you will never enter the kingdom of heaven" (MATTHEW 18:3). This passage has often been cited as the classic expression of spiritual qualifications for the kingdom of God. Such qualities as a childlike sense of dependence, surrender to authority, and open-mindedness and receptivity are lifted

[30] Kyle Haselden, *The Racial Problem in Christian Perspective* (New York, 1959), p. 192.

up as the qualities to which Jesus was referring. Actually Jesus was not referring to spiritual qualities at all. The fact is, children have no qualifications. They receive the kingdom of God as the gift of God on the strength of God's call.

Membership in the Body of Christ belongs to those upon whom it has been bestowed by God's call and election. It is not based on any quality of the person whether racial, cultural, or religious. No man can earn or qualify for membership in the community of faith. The member of God's Church is the recipient of a gift—the call of God and the empowerment of His Spirit. The Church is constituted from above. To belong to it is to be called and sustained from above.

Accordingly, Church members constitute a fellowship of thankful and humble servants of God. They know themselves as the receivers of unmerited gifts. And their lives are urged by gratitude and directed toward thankful obedience. They are no longer in search of the means to self-justification. They have been justified by the forgiving love of God, and the righteousness of Christ has been imputed to them. Since their lives are released from bondage to the self, they constitute a community of service to the kingdom of God. They are not a community of worldly interest and purpose. Togetherness is grounded in their common surrender to Christ, not in social congeniality and common club life.

The ministry of the Church to the world is grounded in its own nature when it is truly the ministry of the Word of God. In the field of race relations the Church has been outstandingly reluctant to utter its own Word. Frequently it has appealed to the conclusions of the social sciences and the humanitarian ideals of the culture, but the relationship of these to biblical faith has often been established only in platitude. When the Church speaks of human rights, it rarely goes beyond the commonly accepted rationalistic understanding of human rights. It fails to accept the responsibility for establishing the theological basis of human rights. Even when the Church speaks of human dignity, a Christian doctrine of man often does not undergird the idea; rather, there are vague references to "American traditions" and "the American way."

The major failure of many Churches to proclaim the Word of God in the present crisis is their direct appeal to the word of the state as the only relevant word. Immediately following the Supreme Court decision of 1954, "obedience to the law of the land" became the ground of decision and the motive for action promulgated by many Churches. In more recent years, there has been a swing away from "law and order" to the gospel message, but many Churches still have not made the swing.

In recent years the Churches have also indicated an increasing awareness that racial hostility is a structured social and political system. For a long time the individualistic illusions of Protestants stood in the way of this awareness. But even this important growth in understanding is not enough. The Churches must also grasp the extent and degree in which the racist faith has permeated cultural institutions and ideas. Christians like to make the claim that in Western civilization large numbers of people, who lack the genuine faith commitment and may even be indifferent, nevertheless live on the "moral capital" of Christianity. Unfortunately, the devotees of the racist faith are able to make the same boast. Racism permeates American life so deeply and comprehensively that it may be thought of as an important element in the "American way of life." Racism is "in the air." In one way or the other, it influences the daily decisions and expectations of persons who harbor only a mild, conformist form of prejudice or may even be "liberal." For example, time and again protests against the exclusion of Negroes from participation in institutional functions and processes have evoked the cry from "liberals" that "we simply did not think about the Negroes." This admission corresponds perfectly with a condition which the racist system has imposed on the Negro—namely, that of a nonentity. Racism must be expurgated from American culture. It is so diffused in the atmosphere that those who sincerely will to be healthy are obliged to breathe in a poisonous environment. The Churches must address themselves to the task of the transformation of cultural values and expectations. Obviously, the Churches stand condemned in their own segregated life, but they cannot wait to be purged of sin before they proclaim the Word of God to a sinful world. The Church alone is the bearer of the Word. No other community has been commissioned to proclaim it. And the same Word which is addressed to the world is addressed to the Church.

D. The renewed individual in racist society

The renewed individual in a racist society is obviously a person with basically the same commitment as the renewed individual in any society. But renewal in a racist society involves also the peculiar experience of deliverance from the special bondages and false perspectives imposed and inculcated by the racist faith.

In matters pertaining to the fundamental questions of human existence—such as creation, fall, and renewal—Christian faith knows of only one race: the human race. It affirms that the whole human kind is alienated from its Creator. This is its fall. And this means that human existence as such is involved in the rebellion against God. There is no factor or virtue in man—natural, rational, or spiritual—which is depraved. It is the whole man who has rebelled against his Creator, and there is no power of restoration within him. In his alienated state, man lives "unto death." He can be rescued only if he surrenders to help which comes from God. Above all, he must be rescued from the false centers of meaning and value which his anxious self-centeredness has prompted him to construct in the delusion that he could guarantee his own security.

The racist self, which identifies itself with wisdom and virtue, must be confronted by the Christ who is, in truth, wisdom and virtue. Only when the sinful, self-centered self is shattered and destroyed can it be renewed. Man becomes aware of the true source and center of life when he is confronted by the power and holiness of God through Christ. Newness of life does not consist in the extension or intensification of human powers, whether these powers be natural, mental, or spiritual. Newness of life has its beginnings neither in the prior inclinations of the new man nor in a budding sense of obligation. Renewal has its source solely in the action of God through Christ. "I have been crucified with Christ; it is no longer I who live, but Christ who lives in me; and the life I now live in the flesh I live by faith in the Son of God, who loved me and gave himself for me" (GALATIANS 2:20).

Christian faith proclaims a wholly new type of righteousness. The righteousness of the man of faith is not his own. His righteousness is outside himself, but must continuously come to himself as one possessed rather than possessing. Christ is the righteousness of the regenerated man; Christ is his new self. The life of grace proceeds from God. Being grasped, the man of faith receives grace and redirection. The renewed life is thus freed from self-seeking because its power is the grace of God and its goal is sonship. God is the center of the picture. The striving after the false securities of the self is overcome; and that center in whom alone man comes to himself is found.

> The true being of man can never be indicated by a human quality, but only—as is implied in the expression "to be in faith"—by the actual state of his relation to God. . . . "True being" means "being in Christ," for "Christ is my righteousness." God's Being in Christ, however—once again not as a quality but as act—is His

> being in love. The true being of man therefore can mean nothing else than standing in the love of God, being drawn into His love of man. Or, to put it differently; it means living a life which from its source in God is directed towards man, towards the interests of others.[31]

The distinctive virtue of the new life is love. But love is not a human acquisition. The new man loves because he has been and is loved. The renewed life loves with the love wherewith it has been loved. Hatred, fear, and anxiety are removed from it because it is grasped by love, wisdom, and power. The racist self is transformed from the state of hostility, fear, and anxiety for itself, because it lives in the security of the love of God, knowing for the first time the fullness of God's covenant community and hoping for the first time for the redemption of all creation.

In the life of faith, the racist also finds a new form of self-affirmation. Racism is inherently an expression of the will to power and glory. It is the purest form of self-glory, for it exalts human being over human being. Christian self-affirmation differs not only from the naked and unashamed self-glory which is racism; it differs also from all philosophical forms of self-affirmation which regard reason as the essence of man. All humanistic forms of self-realizationism promise self-fulfillment through striving and acquisition. Christian self-affirmation is the grateful acceptance and love of ourselves as divine gifts. In the life of faith, self-affirmation takes the form of self-surrender. To affirm ourselves aright is to affirm ourselves in accordance with the divine purpose. Self-affirmation is the dedication of our lives to God; it is not a form of striving. Correspondingly, true self-negation means to be "crucified in Christ." Thus the selfish ego dies. The "I" turns away from itself to the "Thou."

Finally, the pride of racism is overcome by faith. The Christian man is one who feels poor in the Spirit (cf. MATTHEW 5:3). He who has been grasped by the power of God possesses a new clarity concerning the distance between himself and God; his frailty and dependence are clear to him for the first time. In contrast to the arrogance, independence, and self-sufficiency of his former condition, the transformed racist "hungers and thirsts" after the righteousness which can only come by the empowerment of grace. Having experienced the transforming power of grace, the new man knows that there is no level of life at which man possesses his security and fulfillment within himself.

[31] Emil Brunner, *The Divine Imperative* (Philadelphia, 1947), p. 164.

Even when life is organized from beyond the center of the self, it is dependent life and continues to "stand in need of prayer." The renewed life in Christ cannot yield to complacency and self-satisfaction, for it knows that sin prompts men to pride on the very basis of their relation to God, their knowledge of His will, and their approval of what is excellent (cf. ROMANS 2:17-18). For the new life, Christ is the captain. He is "the way, and the truth, and the life" (JOHN 14:6); and His kingdom is the transcendent goal of an enduring hope.